Family Business

Innovative On-Site Child Care Since 1983

Malinda Chouinard

Jennifer Ridgeway

patagonia®

At Patagonia, we publish a collection of books that reflect our pursuits and our values—books on wilderness, outdoor sports, innovation, and a commitment to environmental activism.

© 2016 Patagonia Works

Photo Editors: Cameron Tambakis and Jennifer Ridgeway
Book Designer: Mary Jo Thomas
Editors: Carin Dewhirst Knutson and Nicole Marie
Project Manager: Hilary McLeod
Production: Jordan Damron, Monique Martinez, and Rafael Dunn
Sign Language Illustrations: John Burgoyne

Front Cover Photos: Ted Tambakis (far left only); Kyle Sparks
Back Cover Photos: Chouinard Collection
End Sheets: Sage Kiedaisch

Hardcover ISBN 978-1-938340-59-8
Library of Congress Control Number 2016940799

Publisher's Cataloging-in-Publication Data
Names: Chouinard, Malinda, author. | Ridgeway, Jennifer, author.
Title: Family business : innovative on-site child care since 1983 / Malinda Chouinard, Jennifer Ridgeway.
Description: First edition. | Ventura, California : Patagonia, [2016] | Includes bibliographical references and index.
Identifiers: ISBN: 978-1-938340-53-6 | LCCN: 2016940799
Subjects: LCSH: Patagonia, Inc.--History. | Employer-supported day care--California. | Work environment--California. | Work and family--United States. | Child care services--United States. | Day care centers--United States. | Child development. | Achievement motivation in children. | Creative ability in children. | BISAC: FAMILY & RELATIONSHIPS / Babysitting, Day Care & Child Care. | BUSINESS & ECONOMICS / Workplace Culture.
Classification: LCC: HF5549.5.D39 C46 2016 | DDC: 331.26/6--dc23

First Edition
Printed in British Columbia, Canada, on 100% post-consumer recycled paper. Bound in Arizona, U.S.A.

For 31 years, *Anita Garaway-Furtaw has been the director of Patagonia's Great Pacific Child Development Center. She has awakened joy, creativity, and knowledge in over 1,500 children and counseled countless parents with her patient wisdom.*

In celebration of all Anita has done, we dedicate this book to her.

Anita with her husband, Paul, and son, David. **1985**

About the Family Business project

Patagonia has invested in on-site, corporate-sponsored child care for over three decades. What the company has learned about children, child care, and supporting working families is chronicled in this book and in a series of videos.

The videos can be watched at Patagonia.com/familybusiness. They address issues important to working families and us all: *Patagonia Supports Paid Leave; We Can Be Both: Mothers at Work; Finding Balance: Fathers at Work - Part One; Finding Balance: Fathers at Work - Part Two; Family Business: Raising the Business Case; Outside the Lines: Creative Play; The Rewards of Risk: Building Confidence in Kids*.

To create this book, we reviewed over 85,000 photos, 30,000 of them taken by our staff photographer Kyle Sparks. We also looked at photographs taken by teachers, parents, friends, and freelance photographers over the years. Patagonia photography, both old and new, inspired us during the writing process. The outdoor images remind us of the importance of getting our kids out into nature, so we included photos from our past catalogs and note them in the captions.

Family Business is a book in two parts. Part One tells why Patagonia has invested in on-site child care. Part Two shows how Patagonia's mission and values are put into practice at the Great Pacific Child Development Center (GPCDC).

— *Malinda Chouinard and Jennifer Ridgeway*

THE FREE BOX
WILL WORK
IF WE
★SORT CONTRIBUTIONS
★LEAVE NOTHING ON THE SIDEWALK
★USE THE EXCHANGE BOARD FOR LARGE ITEMS
★BE NEAT
LOVE IT
FREE EXCHANGE
Guild 1000
BOOKS
The Other Side of Midnight
Sidney Sheldon
BABIES

Contents

Why did a clothing company open one of the first corporate-sponsored on-site child-care programs?

– Part One –

Who is taking care of the children? In almost two-thirds of married-couple families, both parents work. In single-parent families, the percentage of working parents is even higher. As the gap between the rich and working poor yawns ever wider, working families increasingly struggle to find quality child care.

The solution is in the place where parents go every day—their workplace. Providing on-site child care for the well-being of the workforce should be simply another normal operational business function. Quality child care that focuses on child development is essential to the future workforce for corporations.

Any company competent enough to recruit experts in design, research, information technology, customer service, shipping, and production knows how to find and hire professionals. Universities around the world train and certify brilliant child development specialists. There is no reason for not having an on-site child-care program at any medium-size, or larger, business.

Patagonia has offered quality on-site child care since 1983. We're happy to serve as a model for other companies. On-site child care, especially for infants, is a necessary element of doing business in our time.

It's why we've written this book.

Why should business care about families?

Weighing the Business Case

To support our families, Patagonia provides company-paid health care and sick time for all employees, paid maternity and paternity leave, access to on-site child care for employees at our headquarters in Ventura and at our Reno distribution center, and financial support to those who need it, among other benefits. In particular, offering on-site child care, we believe, is the right thing to do for employees, working parents, and the life of the workplace. However, a reasonable businessperson might ask, "What does it cost?" It's expensive, if you offer high-quality care and subsidize your employees' tuition. But not as expensive as you'd think.

When President Obama recognized Patagonia CEO Rose Marcario as a Champion of Change for Working Families, Rose accepted the honor on behalf of Patagonia.

The poet Maya Angelou said, "When you know better, you do better," but despite everything we know about the tangible and intangible benefits of taking care of our working families, collectively, we American business leaders provide paid family leave to just 11 percent of U.S. workers. As of April 2016, three states and the District of Columbia offer paid family leave: California, New Jersey, and Rhode Island.

The United States is one of only two countries in the industrialized world that offers no federal paid maternity leave. And every day in America, most women return to work after the birth of a child to find an unsupportive environment lacking on-site child care, lactation programs, and paid medical leave.

We don't have to scratch our heads and wonder why there is an alarming lack of women in positions of leadership, boardrooms, and public office. Women will never be able to effectively "lean in" without the proper economic, social, and community support for the most critical work of all: raising the next generation.

The good news for skeptical business leaders: Supporting our working families isn't just the ethical thing to do (which, frankly, should be all we need if we are to be responsible leaders), it will also balance out

financially. This book focuses on Patagonia's 33-year commitment to providing on-site child care at our headquarters in Ventura, California, but research showing the business benefits of paid family and medical leave and other critical programs is abundant.

For now, let me illustrate the basic math that gives me confidence as Patagonia's chief executive not only to provide on-site child care to our parents at our headquarters, but, as of this year, to expand it to our 400-employee distribution center in Reno, Nevada, as well.

Tax Benefits—Costs Recouped: 50%

The federal government recognizes the value of on-site child care to both working parents and the economy and grants a qualified child-care program a yearly tax credit of $150,000. In addition, the government allows a company to deduct 35 percent of its unrecovered costs from its corporate tax bite.

Employee Retention—Costs Recouped: 30%

Turnover costs (of losing an employee and training a replacement) include lost productivity while the position is vacant, plus recruitment, relocation, and training time. This can range from 35 percent of annual salary for a nonmanagerial employee, to 125 percent of salary for a manager, to a couple of years' pay for a director or vice president. In the United States, 20–35 percent of working mothers who give birth never return to their previous job.

At Patagonia, for the past five years, we've seen 100 percent of moms return to work after maternity leave. Moreover, the availability of on-site child care remains important for allowing mothers to breast-feed infants on demand. For the past five years, our turnover rate for parents who have children in the program has run 25 percent less than for our general employee population.

Employee Engagement—Costs Recouped: 11%

The term *engagement* is used to measure wholeheartedness, or how an employee feels about his or her job and employer. Higher engagement creates higher levels of customer satisfaction and business performance. Studies indicate that when parents have access to high-quality, on-site child care at work, they are more engaged—even more so than colleagues as a whole—and that increased engagement means the company does better financially.

People don't have to choose between paying bills and seeing their kids shine in the class play. And that means that that worker will do whatever it takes to help the company the next time out because they know that Rose and others at the very top are looking out for them. — *President Barack Obama, April, 15, 2015*

Bottom Line—Costs Recouped: 91%

In sum, we estimate that we recover 91 percent of our calculable costs annually. We're not alone. JPMorgan Chase Bank, N.A., has estimated returns of 115 percent for its child-care program; global business consultant KPMG found that its clients earned a return on investment (ROI) of 125 percent.

Of course, this quantifiable picture leaves out the obvious intangible benefits of providing on-site child care. All told, we would say that an ROI of 115 percent or 125 percent on our own program would not surprise us. Benefits in the intangible category include:

— More women in management. Studies show a healthy gender mix at the leadership level makes business smarter and more creative and improves performance. At Patagonia, women make up 50 percent of our workforce, including roughly half of upper management positions.

— Greater employee loyalty. Providing high-quality, on-site child care helps a business exercise its obligations as an employer and community citizen. Such businesses earn the trust of their employees, who give their time more wholeheartedly, and the loyalty of customers, who will buy from a brand, all else being equal, with the better reputation.

— Stronger workplace culture of trust. At Patagonia, if you ask parents the benefit of having their child on-site, they might tell you what a difference it makes to be able to check in, have lunch together, and be freed from the complications stemming from dropping off and picking up the child elsewhere. If you ask a nonparent the greatest benefit of having the kids around, he or she might tell you that having kids around reminds us, parents and nonparents alike, that we are behaving for real in a real world, and not just hired guns asked to leave our deepest selves behind the moment the workday starts.

For 33 years, Patagonia has provided on-site child care: a mandate from our founders, who believed it was a moral imperative. Even in times of economic struggle, the program was never cut, because they believed in providing a supportive work environment for working families. Taking care of our tribe is part of our culture and our commitment to helping our own people live the way they want.

It's true, there are financial costs to offering on-site child care, and they can be expensive if you offer high-quality programs or subsidize your employees' tuition when on-site care is not available. But the benefits—financial and otherwise—pay for themselves every year. As a CEO, it's not even a question in my mind. Business leaders (and their chief financial officers) should take note.

CEOs of Esprit, Doug Tompkins and Peter Buckley, along with Yvon Chouinard are amazed by pint-size potties for the soon-to-be-opened child-care center at Patagonia headquarters. Ventura, California. **1984**

Benefits recouped as a percentage of costs of on-site child care

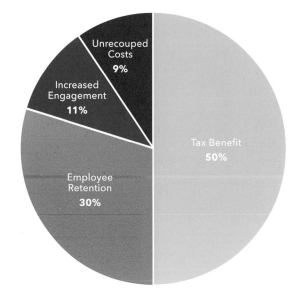

Unrecouped Costs 9%

Increased Engagement 11%

Tax Benefit 50%

Employee Retention 30%

Patagonia Design Team, 2016

A master in the art of living draws no sharp distinction between his work and his play; his labor and his leisure; his mind and his body; his education and his recreation. He hardly knows which is which. He simply pursues his vision of excellence through whatever he is doing. — *L. P. Jacks*

Why did we think on-site child care was a good idea in 1983?

Three Perspectives: The History of Patagonia's On-Site Child-Care Program

Patagonia is a tribe of storytellers, and what follows is the three-part tale about the beginnings of the Great Pacific Child Development Center (GPCDC). Each of our three storytellers brings her perspective to the saga. We start with Malinda Chouinard, who believes that "If bozos like us can start a child-care program, then anyone can." Next, GPCDC's co-founder and Patagonia's first Director of Marketing, Jennifer Ridgeway, describes the role her own disruptive newborn (she was a wailer) played in the formation of our on-site child care. And between these two stories, Kris Tompkins, Patagonia's first CEO, shares her perspective on the need for and the benefits of providing support for working families.

"Whether trekking in Nepal or taking care of business in the Commonwealth of Dominica, not everyone was happy following parents around at work, airports, and elsewhere." —*Malinda Chouinard*

Malinda looks back to the early days of Patagonia and recounts what prompted her to create an on-site corporate-sponsored child-care program.

1 In the early 1970s, I married Yvon Chouinard, the only climber I knew with a real job. Since 1957, Yvon had been selling his hand-forged climbing hardware. We lived and worked with climbers and surfers in and around the old Smith-Hobson warehouse in Ventura, California. That's where the Chouinard Equipment for alpinists blacksmith shop was—in a tin shed.

We rented a single-walled cabin on a Ventura surf break in the winters. When the owners returned each summer, we moved back into the blacksmith shop.

2 Camping out on the loading dock from May to October almost coincided with my job teaching art and home economics at the local high school. The timing also determined Yvon's summer migration to climb in Yosemite, the Canadian Rockies, and Wyoming.

None of this was a problem. We were young, and climbers have always been migratory, following the seasons to climb, surf, fish, ski, and kayak. I was well-suited to this life. As the child of a Pan Am pilot and flight engineer, my family moved every year—in 1959, we moved six times.

3 In 1972, things changed for us. Our Ventura landlord, Fred Smith, presented a unique opportunity: He would sell his property, which included the tin shed we rented and the old abandoned slaughterhouse/warehouse in front. He even offered to carry the mortgage for the same price as the rent.

Along with our partners Dorene and Tom Frost, we became owners of buildings in dire need of restoration, so I quit my teaching job to join my brother-in-law, Jeff, in a year-long do-it-yourself remodel. The first thing I did was cobble together an apartment in the warehouse basement. This was a big improvement over sleeping under the packing bench.

1

2

3

4

The corner office of the warehouse eventually became our first retail store, Great Pacific Iron Works. Yvon had always sold his climbing equipment—pitons and carabiners—from his car, via mail order, and from the blacksmith shop. To his climbing gear, we added some clothing and supplies for backpackers and then opened a real store. The dilapidated and cavernous building provided plenty of room.

4 We learned to design and sew clothing and packs upstairs above the new shipping bins. As a global climber, Yvon was often away climbing. After our children were born, he was gone many months during the year. His job was to design, make, and test the gear he used for climbing. It took the better part of eight winters of research and testing to develop the gear for his book *Climbing Ice*. There are no ice climbs near Ventura.

5

5   In 1974, when our partners brought their newborn to work, none of us knew anything about babies. The next year, when I moved my own baby into the retail office, not everyone was happy. All these years later, I am still mortified to recall the sudden wardrobe failure that exposed me and my nursing newborn to a startled retail customer.

6

6   I had worked on my own for years, and I knew I could take care of myself, but nothing prepared me for the isolation and exhaustion of being a working mother.

7   My parents lived six hours away and often took over the babysitting during our longer work trips. In those days, the airlines allowed our three-year-old to fly unaccompanied to visit his grandparents.

7

The presence of dirty diapers caused the retail store manager to declare one morning, "It's me or the baby!" Abruptly, like most working mothers, I was forced to make a choice. Without alternatives, I began working from home—and from the road. — *Malinda Chouinard*

8   Everyone became a babysitter. Once during a meeting, I handed my newborn to a colleague. When I returned moments later, my breast-fed baby was eagerly sucking up a fast-food chocolate milk shake.

9   Yvon has been doing business in Japan since the late 1960s. So our nursing newborn came along to Japan, Nepal, Hong Kong, and Germany.

10 Working in Japan at our wholesale dealer's store with a very jet-lagged baby.

11 A baby can be a liability for a professional mountain climber. Today, Patagonia's nursing babies still travel with their mothers, but their beloved Patagonia primary caregivers accompany them, paid for by the company.

12　When we needed a trade show booth in the '70s, I made and shipped it while taking care of our two very young children.

13

14

13 At times Patagonia has been almost all women, many with children. But many of the employees were also unmarried, carefree athletes. One especially crazy week at work, I decided I needed a babysitter for my toddler. I found and hired a transient camper from the classified section of the newspaper. I spent the week terrified I would return home to a ransom note. Keeping up at work became increasingly impossible.

It was evident that the few other working parents were having as hard a time as I was. When several of my divorced colleagues lost custody of their young children due to lack of child care, my personal struggle became a "workers' struggle." Emboldened, I began to make unilateral decisions for which I had no budget, no authority, and zero preparation.

14 In January of 1983, without a thought as to whether it was suitable for child care, I ordered a trailer and put it in the parking lot. It was for an infant who had had a difficult birth and needed to be close to her mother. That same year, with a new building under construction, I made an unauthorized architectural change to install little sinks and toilets in a back corner, creating a space so children could have their own area with babysitters to watch over them.

In January of 1984, we opened our on-site child care center in the new building. Only then did I discover that there were laws pertaining to child care in a workplace. There were no infant-care facilities in Ventura at that time, only a few part-time church preschools. Church preschools had to follow certain rules, and we discovered they applied to us, too.

15 Luckily, the newly appointed Commission on Women, under the authority of the Ventura County Board of Supervisors, came to our rescue by walking us through the required permits. The process seemed like an eternity to the scrambling parents.

On March 25, 1984, the *Ventura County Star-Free Press* (now *Ventura County Star*) ran a story about the opening of the center, which included our goals:

— It is our desire to reduce wasted childhoods, which we believe is the norm for the American child today. A child's work is play. It is not a child's work to be taught; it is his work to learn. It is not valuable for children to spend their days being entertained; it is their job to use their imagination, and in doing so not only learn, but enjoy themselves.

— Americans confuse toys with playing, teachers with learning, and parenting with supervising. Children in a happy home spend hours frittering away time, watching their parents, thinking, experimenting, testing, and exploring. That is what we hope you will see our children doing. We want our environment to challenge the children to do these things in a calm, natural, homelike, happy atmosphere.

— Our third goal is to show the children quite a different view of adults from that portrayed on TV, not to mention how they see us as we drag in from a long day at work to face tired kids and household tasks. Children seldom get to watch adults at work, which is where most of us are at our best—being grown-ups who like themselves and their lives. Each of us is now a role model.

15

Children at home with on-site day care

By Jane Nolan

Elizabeth Murphy, 7, in top photo, goes for a ride in the play area at Great Pacific Iron Works in Ventura, while her mother is working; the day care arrangement is one of the first at the parent's employment site in Ventura County. Above, at immediate right, Elizabeth and her mother Pam Murphy of Santa Paula share a break at the center. Below right, Eamon Taggart, 4, son of Phil and Damaris Taggart, paints during an art session. At far right, Malinda Chouinard and daughter Claire, 4, celebrate the opening of the company's on-site child care center

What do the kids think?

I walked into our child-care building one day and asked some of the four- and five-year-olds, "Hi, kids! How's school?"

One young guy immediately corrected me. "We're not in school; we're at work. My mother works over there, and I work here."

What a difference that is from your average kid whose father or mother disappears every day for eight hours or more and who thus grows up with no concept of work.

— *Yvon Chouinard*

16 Father and son: Nowadays, they both make and test fishing and surfing equipment.

17 Our on-site child-care center meant that we could test and fit prototypes for the kids' clothing line right downstairs from the design department.

As young children in the 1980s, these two would wander into their moms' design racks. They now work in the same building, and their babies are downstairs in child care.

18

19

18 Parents who spend lots of time outdoors need their children to have the same high-tech clothing that they wear themselves.

19 Caught in a subzero snowstorm one winter evening, we wrapped our baby in her father's prototype pile jacket and stuffed her into a backpack. With great effort, we added a kids'

pile jacket to the adult clothing line. Eventually, a kids' clothing line evolved. Patagonia kids have long taken an active role as durability testers and fit models. Both parents and kids took it upon themselves to design and make what they needed.

Patagonia kids are among our best products. — *Yvon Chouinard*

Trekking to Everest, we discovered that only
our prototype pile jackets kept the baby warm
and dry. Yvon went without. — *Malinda Chouinard*

Kris remembers the days before Patagonia committed to on-site child care.

Coming to work for Yvon and Malinda Chouinard allowed me to work in an environment not likely found in most other places in 1972.

We weren't hippies, but we didn't want to work in a traditional business. Looking back on it today, I realize the values that formed the company—and that I took for granted then—would become the bellwethers for what the most discerning talent is looking for in leading companies anywhere in the world today. And the arrival of babies in our offices was no small part of this cultural revolution.

Malinda was one of the first among us to become a mother, and we took for granted that her son, Fletcher, would come to work each day, swaddled tightly against her chest or bobbing along against her back. It was the 1970s, and the era of children being seen but not heard was a fading memory. And along came more babies: one sleeping soundly tucked under a desk, another sleeping next to her

mother, who was busy editing photographs for our catalogs. There were babies springing up like tiny fireflies appearing at night. At the time, it seemed logical and right that our founding team members would feel free to bring their babies to work. And the babies were included in just about everything—scooped up and off to meetings around the building or made the center of attention during lunchtime. I became quite good at keeping Fletcher on my lap while hammering away on sales projections with our reps and sales team. It all seemed quite normal, and certainly it all seemed quite right. Those who didn't have babies usually had a dog. I remember quite clearly walking into the Great Pacific Iron Works retail store for a meeting and finding two black Labrador puppies asleep in one of our tents on the sales floor and a baby sleeping peacefully in a chair next to the cash register. I remember thinking, *Someday I will have to write about this.*

When Malinda decided to open the company's child-care center it was a jarring idea—the kids wouldn't be scattered throughout the buildings anymore, and the idea of a child-care center was very new. I didn't know what to make of it. Fortunately, she persevered, and we spent the next few years trying to find the money in our annual budgets to support it. Finally having funding gave Malinda enough room to create what had long been on her mind—a fully active child-care center integrated into the company. As it turns out, it was a very wise business decision.

When small kids are within earshot of our working day, something quite tangible happens: Language changes in the presence of babies. We are our best and most loving selves in the presence of babies and toddlers, and there is some invisible lasso that ties all of us more firmly together as our work lives dovetail with our personal lives.

Today, the top companies in the world are managed in ways that would have been unimaginable even 15 years ago. The best students coming out of graduate schools are looking for companies that are leading in more ways than simply a finely tuned bottom line. In this same spirit, we hope this book may become a bellwether for companies to change the relationship among business, family, and raising healthy, well-rounded children.

Patagonia's prototype of on-site child care: CEO Kris McDivitt Tompkins holds an employee's baby during a sales meeting. **1980**

Chouinard Equipment's first retail store was in the smithy's shipping room. Ventura, California. **1974**

We are our best and most loving selves in the presence of babies and toddlers, and there is some invisible lasso that ties all of us more firmly together as our work lives dovetail with our personal lives. — *Kris McDivitt Tompkins*

It was the birth of Jennifer's first child that led to the establishment of on-site child care at Patagonia in the early 1980s.

The best way to inspire others is through sharing stories, and my story starts in 1981 when the CEO of fledgling Patagonia, Kris McDivitt (later Tompkins), decided I should become the Director of Marketing and Advertising. I said, "I don't know anything about marketing and advertising." Kris replied, "Neither does anyone else around here."

Patagonia's single warehouse building was surrounded by oil-field supply companies and an adjacent café whose patrons were mostly members of the local chapter of the Hells Angels biker club. I shared with (also newly hired) Art Director Kathy Ryan (later Metcalf) a tiny, airless, windowless space that we referred to as The Box. With Yvon and Kris, we put together the first Patagonia catalogs with those quirky, often extreme photographs of climbers, kayakers, mountaineers, skiers, surfers, fly fishermen and women, sailors, and trail runners—real people in real situations. Unique for the time, we shaped what became Patagonia's version of marketing.

In The Box during the summer of 1982, temperatures hovered around 110 degrees, and I was eight months pregnant. A climber

joined Kathy and me in our office to write copy for Chouinard Equipment, so now it was really tight. He ceaselessly made himself sandwiches with Miracle Whip on Wonder Bread which kept me in a perpetual state of nausea.

I worked until the day before our daughter was born. At that time, there was no paid maternity leave at Patagonia or in the state of California (both now offer paid leave). It didn't really matter, because there was no one to take on "marketing and advertising" anyway. So after a three-week leave due to a cesarean, I optimistically went back to work with my new daughter Carissa tucked in a bassinet under my desk. I presumed she would follow the lead of previously content Patagonia working mothers' babies.

It never occurred to any of us that this might not work out. Our daughter, perhaps due to a high-stress birth, was, as some of my coworkers who preferred dogs described her, "a wailer." No one in the entire building—sales, accounting, marketing, warehousing, shipping—could have a phone conversation. No one could have a one-on-one conversation. Clearly, the pacified sleeping baby in the bassinet or backpack was not my baby.

Local options for infant care in the area were limited and dismal. Out of desperation, my newly widowed mother (who in retrospect was a saint) would drive with me to work and stroll Carissa around the neighborhood as the Hells Angels roared by, then bring her to me to nurse in the car. This proved neither a safe nor a pleasant solution. I tried leaving Carissa at home with my mother. I wanted to breast-feed her, so I expressed milk at work in a corner of the retail store's storage basement—but the store manager objected, pointed at me, and said, "You should be at home with your baby."

I loved my work, and I had to work, but I couldn't figure out exactly what to do. Being an integral part of a quickly evolving company was exciting. In addition, I was married to expedition climber, free-lance photographer, and filmmaker Rick Ridgeway, one of the first Americans to climb K2, which translates to "gone a lot" ... he was gone six to nine months out of the year. Much of the time, I was basically a single-though-married working mother, and meeting my baby's needs was my first priority.

Malinda had a brainstorm: She rented a trailer, put it in the parking lot, and installed a rocking chair and a crib. It was January 1983. My mother came to work with me and stayed in the trailer to take

care of Carissa, who was now three months old. Carissa was happy with the new arrangement. I could spend time with her throughout the day and nurse her on-site. Soon it seemed like a good idea to have other employees' kids who were in need of child care join them. So Malinda hired a babysitter to work alongside my mother. "The Trailer" was the company's first on-site child care.

1   The pacified sleeping baby under the desk in the bassinet or in the backpack was not MY baby. **1982**

2   Being able to nurse your baby and spend time with him or her throughout the day is of incomparable value. **1983**

3   Patagonia headquarters is only a few blocks from the beach, so parents can take their kids out for lunchtime walks. **1984**

A new building was under construction, and when it opened a year later, Malinda made certain it included indoor and outdoor spaces for child care. For the first year, it was like on-site babysitting for kids ranging in age from toddlers to eight-year-olds. It was chaotic. Sometimes it was like something out of *Lord of the Flies*.

It became clear we needed a child care professional to step in. For several frustrating months, we interviewed one candidate after another. Finally, in June 1985, we interviewed Anita Garaway-Furtaw. We begged her to start immediately. One week later, she replaced most of the staff with credentialed professionals, and chaos gave way to order, structure, and philosophy. One of Anita's initial moves says it all: She changed the name of the nascent center from Great Pacific Day Care to Great Pacific Child Development Center (GPCDC). That was 30 years ago. Since then, over 1,500 children have passed through the gates.

Our three children grew up lovingly nurtured right there with me at Patagonia. It is hard to calculate the value of working in a joyful and supportive environment surrounded by people who feel like family while being in close proximity to your growing child. It is profound and tribal—it feels like a village, because it *is* a village. Often when people visit Patagonia's headquarters, they comment on how much the company feels like a family, and we point out that is because it looks like a family—kids in the playground next to the reception and outdoor lunch area—and sounds like a family—the laughter of the kids playing carries into the office buildings surrounding the playground. When your child physically knows your work, your child is psychologically part of your work. It operates both ways because each child grows up understanding the job you do. The entire Patagonia community takes part in watching your child grow up, and the child has an impact on their lives. In our view, that is the definition of family.

4   The Patagonia GPCDC play yard. **1985**

5 Halloween at Patagonia is a tradition: CEO Kris McDivitt (Tompkins) with Carissa. **1984**

6 Carissa got an early start in graphic design by creating her own catalogs, in the cut-and-paste era, from vendors' samples at my desk. **1985**

7 Messy outdoor play has always been a key philosophy of Patagonia's child-care program. **1986**

8 It's such a treat to have lunch with your kids in the middle of the day out at the picnic tables. **1989**

Education is a natural process carried out by the child and is not acquired by listening to words, but by experiences in the environment. — *Dr. Maria Montessori*

Carissa's daughter, two-year-old Coda, is at GPCDC, with her grandfather and aunt working on-site and her mother working as a filmmaker. Many employees who as children attended GPCDC now work at Patagonia and joyfully take their babies straight to work with them after their maternity or paternity leave. I only wish every working parent in America were as fortunate.

9   The kids at Patagonia spend over half of their time playing outdoors without specific teacher-directed activities. **1989**

10   Aunt Cameron stops by GPCDC for face painting with Coda. **2016**

11   Coda helping her mother edit the video *We Can Be Both: Mothers at Work.* **2016**

12   My husband, Rick Ridgeway, VP of Public Engagement, and Coda arrive at Patagonia for a day of play and work. **2016**

How can business care for families?

– Part Two –

The past 33 years and over 1,500 children have taught us lessons about child development and running a child-care center.

In this section, Chapter One summarizes GPCDC's trajectory over the past three decades. Chapter Two outlines the foundation of the program: our guiding philosophies and key practices, which reflect Patagonia's values, mission, and culture.

Chapters Three through Thirteen illustrate how our principles are put into practice each day as we care for infants, toddlers, and young children. We describe the intricacies of child development and capture our perspective on how to best support the growing child. In the final chapter, Chapter Fourteen, we consider the future of Patagonia's child-care programs and where to go from here.

left: Assistant Photo Editors (both three-years-old) say, "THAT does NOT look like a good idea!" Spring Catalog 1995 *— Greg Epperson*

How did Patagonia go from babysitting in a trailer to a child development center?

Chapter One: 33 Years of Lessons Learned

Refining the practices and philosophy of Patagonia's child-care center has been an ongoing task for the past 33 years. *Quality* is one of Yvon Chouinard's core values, and it is also a core value of our center. But what should quality look like? How will we know when we are successful? Over the years, what we've considered *quality* regarding our child-care program has evolved.

In the early days, establishing any kind of child care was a challenge, so having a place for children at all seemed the pinnacle of quality. To understand how we've created a high-quality, on-site, corporate-sponsored child-care program, one needs to understand where we started.

Anita was the first experienced, qualified director of Patagonia's child-care center and was known as the program's fairy godmother who could solve any problem.

1980s—Urgent need for child care at Patagonia

I wasn't around for the early days of child care at Patagonia, but I've heard stories. In the late '70s and early '80s, Patagonia employees struggled to balance work and family. In those days, employees brought their babies to work and kept them under their desks or, as the children got older, let them run free around the Patagonia offices and grounds. But problems arose, and something had to be done.

Malinda Chouinard took steps to solve the child-care issue but has often lamented to me, "We had no idea what we were doing. At first, it was just a babysitting service in a trailer." The Patagonia day-care program kept growing and moved into its own building in 1984.

While many parenting problems were solved, there was one more mishap. On the first day of school, a parent accidentally forgot to pick up their child. Malinda immediately bought a van, hiding the cost in the shipping department budget. From that moment on, Patagonia has provided after-school pickup for children in kindergarten through third grade.

From babysitting service to Great Pacific Child Development Center

When asked to start immediately as the Director of Patagonia's Great Pacific Day Care (as it was called then), I jumped right in. Equipped with undergraduate and graduate degrees in early childhood education and 14 years combined experience as a teacher and child center director, I started work Monday, June 10, 1985. The day-care center had been open over a year, and my first goal was to get the program compliant with California Department of Social Services (DSS) rules.

1   Anita Garaway-Furtaw, GPCDC's first director, has always had a magic touch with infants, able to soothe them in minutes. **1985**

2   The famous first van: Since 1984, we have had after-school pickup. **1984**

I made the following changes immediately:

— Instituted a formal program based on best practices in child development

— Brought the center into full compliance with DSS regulations

— Created clearly defined procedures and changed the noncommittal tuition structure

— Changed the name from Great Pacific Day Care to Great Pacific Child Development Center (GPCDC)

The parents embraced these changes and supported the program wholeheartedly, and soon the program expanded to include a preschool.

Higher standards: RIE and NAEYC accreditation

I wanted to base our infant and preschool programs on sound philosophy and practices, so I contacted Resources for Infant Educarers (RIE) in Los Angeles to train the GPCDC staff. RIE was founded by Magda Gerber, the world-renowned expert in infant caregiving who advocates that infants be allowed to develop at their own pace. In 1986, Magda became my teacher, and she coached me, saying, "Anita, sit on your hands to remind yourself to slow down and just watch. The babies will tell you what they need."

RIE training galvanized and united our staff around the following principles:

— The importance of respecting children

— The critical importance of play in each child's development

— The need for language-rich environments

The National Association for the Education of Young Children (NAEYC) sets standards for early-childhood programs and provides accreditation. Receiving accreditation is an arduous process as programs are evaluated on everything from teacher qualifications to school environment—NAEYC publishes a 132-page booklet to help centers prepare for accreditation. In 1988, it was an honor to become one of the first centers in Ventura County to receive NAEYC accreditation. Because of this, other programs and companies began contacting GPCDC for advice.

5

3   We follow many tenets of the RIE philosophy: Infants are placed on their backs and can move and develop at their own pace, in their own time.

4   Listening carefully demonstrates respect and often means meeting children at their level.

5   Reading books aloud to children builds literacy skills and is an integral part of a language-rich environment.

1990s–GPCDC becomes a resource for others and advocates for early childhood education

While working at GPCDC, I taught a class called "Child Growth and Development" for California Lutheran University's teacher preparation program. Educating new teachers, I had the opportunity to match current child development theories with best practices. I encouraged student teachers who were "observing and getting their hours" to come to GPCDC. I offered apprenticeships, which helped improve our programs. In some cases, we ended up hiring these students.

On-site corporate-sponsored child care was still an anomaly in the 1990s and drew a lot of attention from local politicians. Many came to visit GPCDC. One congressman brought a colleague from Connecticut to visit who was intrigued by the idea of linking outstanding child-care centers with high-quality in-home child care providers. Eventually, I traveled to Washington, DC, and worked to help draft legislation to develop pilot projects nationwide to improve child care. This was when I started advocating for better child care at the national level.

National attention turns to early childhood education

In the mid-1990s, several studies underscored the importance of high-quality early childhood education:

— A 1995 report revealed that most child-care programs in the United States were mediocre. This study linked "… high-quality child care to children's achievement of higher cognitive and social skills that help them prepare for kindergarten and to succeed in school."

— In 1996, a study provided insights into very young infants' learning capabilities, connecting brain development and children's learning and illustrating the value of quality early care programs for babies.

This research confirmed the positive effects of high-quality child-care centers on child development and validated our efforts to advocate for high-quality child care nationwide.

GPCDC conducts countless tours and answers hundreds of questions from companies interested in starting similar programs. We assist other companies through the licensing process and offer guidance as they hire staff, develop curriculum, and design indoor and outdoor environments.

9

10

11

6 Dianne Feinstein, who would be elected to the United States Senate in 1992, visits Anita at GPCDC. **1990**

7 Our teachers develop trusting, healthy relationships with children, which results in a warm, family-like atmosphere where children can blossom.

8 We believe that children learn best in outdoor environments.

9 Unstructured play allows children to be creative, resourceful, and solve problems independently.

10 Studies done in the 1990s indicate that high-quality early childhood education has a positive impact on cognitive development.

11 In a thoughtfully designed area that allows for all kinds of play, kids can jump, climb, run, or dig.

2000 to the present—We take our program outside and to our Distribution Center in Reno. I pass the baton.

In 2010, many of our teachers received training in the Outdoor Classroom Project (OCP) in Santa Barbara. What they learned transformed GPCDC. Patagonia, as an outdoor gear company, has always understood the benefit of being outside in nature. After OCP training, GPCDC's programs were revamped to increase the quantity and quality of outdoor experiences for our children. It was a significant accomplishment to be chosen as a demonstration site for OCP. We now work to help other centers understand how small changes to their outdoor space can create significant changes in how children learn.

We opened the Truckee River Child Development Center at our Distribution Center in Reno, Nevada, in February 2016. The on-site program serves nursing infants and their families and will soon expand to provide care for children ages three to five in a pre-school classroom.

Lessons learned

Working with young children is often considered an unintellectual pursuit and derogatorily described as "day care" or "babysitting." After decades of providing on-site child care, we've learned that educating young children is both science and art. As a science, it involves intricate knowledge of the many stages of typical development experienced by young children, how those stages fit together, and the ways that information fits with the creation of developmentally and individually appropriate curriculum. Good teachers make all the pieces fit together effortlessly, and that's why teaching is also an art—one that requires finesse, creativity, and imagination.

12   Shown here in our Outdoor Classroom, Susan Welbourn has been with the GPCDC program since 1985.

13   Patagonia's Truckee River Child Development Center opened on-site at our distribution center in Reno, Nevada, in February 2016.

14   *left to right:* Anita Garaway-Furtaw, Director of GPCDC, 1985-2016; Maureen McCarthy, currently Manager of GPCDC, 1987-present; Sheryl Shushan, Director of Global Family Services, started February 2016.

What principles guide our practices?

Chapter Two: Our Philosophy

A key to building a strong program for children and families is a working philosophy—one that outlines tenets that educators and parents can use to inform their actions. Over the past 33 years, we've married Patagonia's values and history with our understanding of child development to create a set of principles that guides our practices.

"Childhood is not a race to see how quickly a child can read, write, and count. It's a small window of time to learn and develop at the pace that is right for each individual child. Earlier is not better." *— Magda Gerber*

Nursing on-site is the bedrock of our program.

Patagonia's breast-feeding and family policies began as frantic solutions for colleagues who were struggling to care for their babies and also keep their jobs. As research mounted showing that mothers and infants benefit physically and emotionally from nursing, we developed systems that encourage families to prolong nursing past the crucial first six months. We educate expecting parents about, among other things, the benefits of breast-feeding. When their babies arrive, all parents (including adopting families) are given paid leave. Mothers returning to work at our Ventura headquarters and Reno distribution center can use private lactation rooms, or anywhere they are comfortable, to feed their babies anytime. Our teachers alert nursing mothers that their babies need them, but if a nursing mother is unable to leave a meeting, her baby is brought to her. Those working in our U.S. retail stores benefit from child-care assistance programs. Still, our employees in the United States don't have the advantages of European colleagues, to which we aspire.

Involved dads from the beginning.

Businesses that provide paternity leave and encourage men to take advantage of it earn employee loyalty, boost retention rates, and have balanced, focused employees. Dads report feeling engaged and happy when they care for their children from the start. When both parents care for a newborn, their bonds deepen, and children benefit emotionally, socially, and cognitively. A recent study by Sarah Thébaud at the University of California, Santa Barbara, found that men and women ages 18 to 32 across all education and income levels felt that men and women should share child raising. But when faced with a lack of family-friendly policies at work, most fell back on traditional roles. Patagonia dads can take their turn at giving the baby a bottle, reading to the child at nap time, etc.

Doing well by doing right by others.

Patagonia employees avoid the hardest decisions American parents must make—such as choosing between keeping a job or caring for a newborn. Not only do both new mothers and fathers take time when their babies are born, but when nursing mothers go on a business trip, Patagonia's Travel Support Program funds the cost of a family member or a GPCDC caregiver to accompany the nursing mom. Supporting employees in times of need—for example, after the birth of a child or a serious family emergency—gives our colleagues strength, and we all learn and gain wisdom together.

Patagonia benefits by investing in on-site child care.

In the 1970s when we were discussing the possibility of founding a child-care center at Patagonia, there were dissenters who didn't want to use Patagonia's "spare cash" to run a school. We did it anyway. What we found was that when new moms can breast-feed their infants, when parents are nearby if their child falls ill, when children develop relationships with their parents' coworkers, our employees stay longer, and our business thrives. Yvon Chouinard wrote in

The Responsible Company: "The presence of kids and the introduction of child care taught us that if there is some quality about the workplace you love and don't want to lose, don't. It costs Patagonia $50,000, on average, to recruit, train, and get up to speed a new employee; if we want to make any money, it's a good idea to keep the ones we have happy and fully engaged."

Believing in the abilities of infants creates competent children.

The Resources for Infant Educarers (RIE) philosophy has always influenced how we work with children. Although we adapt RIE practices, we do believe each child is inherently competent and has the right to be respected as a valuable individual. By being observant and aware, we value each infant, which means he or she grows up self-assured because his or her early impulses were respected. Our belief translates into many practices. For example, we don't put children in physical positions they can't get into or out of on their own. Babies are placed on their backs where they are free to move, rolling from side to side and eventually rolling over. Each child follows a particular sequence of development that marks him or her as unique. We do our best to honor the process.

Struggle is essential to becoming a capable person.

If adults consistently rescue children from safe but uncomfortable situations, children will rely on adult intervention and eventually learn to lack confidence in their abilities. Children are capable of making decisions about their development and know intrinsically that struggle is part of growing up. We all walk through life refining the art of the struggle; it's how we discover what we are capable of.

Every test successfully met is rewarded by some growth in intuitive knowledge, strengthening of character, or initiation into a higher consciousness. — *Paul Brunton*

Small risks build confidence for assessing larger ones.

Patagonia was founded by climbers—risk taking is in our blood. When babies want to roll down the grassy hill or two-year-olds want to scale the climbing wall, we stand nearby and assist only if necessary. When children make relatively small decisions—*Should I jump from this rock?*—they practice weighing consequences before they get older and must make higher-stakes choices. Supporting children in taking chances teaches them to guide themselves safely, thoughtfully, and confidently.

Outdoor, uninterrupted play promotes mental and emotional maturity.

Unstructured play gives children the time they need to develop strong friendships and explore and master their interests, which leads to better problem-solving and social skills. Therefore, teachers support play by keeping a close watch and providing help only when needed. Teachers are honored to be included in child-directed games but recognize that adults influence the imaginative nature of play. Uninterrupted play is tied to children's creativity, and it's their most important pursuit. Dr. Stuart Brown, a psychologist and founder of the National Institute for Play, agrees that children need an environment with "the opportunity to engage in open, free play where they're allowed to self-organize. It's really a central part of being human and developing into competent adulthood … Wild play helps shape who we become, and it should be embraced, not feared."

Conflict teaches problem solving and compassion.

Children spend their days negotiating. Sometimes negotiations go smoothly, and other times not. Conflicts between children aren't the problem; they are full of potential. Karen Stephens, educator and champion of positive discipline, believes, "Valuable social skills are developed as children learn to problem-solve and defuse confrontations. Logical thinking is nurtured as children comprehend rules and reasons for them. When experiencing consequences, children learn about cause and effect. They learn to anticipate and predict events within their control." Teachers use conflict to model effective language and build compassion. They help children mediate conflict until they can do it on their own. There's no better way to engage children, who are motivated by connection with family and friends, than through the trials and pleasures of social life.

Positive discipline gives kids the benefit of the doubt.

I wonder what will happen if I put the goldfish in the toilet? Childhood is a time for imperfect plans and failed experiments. To punish children harshly dampens initiative and creativity, the qualities they need to flourish. Therefore, when children make mistakes, our teachers use language carefully, focus on problem solving, and praise children's positive behavior. Karen Stephens, expert on positive discipline, writes, "When positive discipline is used, caregivers introduce children to the world of relationships with compassion and patience. As a result, children develop social competence. Just as importantly, they learn to trust adults. By being treated with gentleness and high regard, they learn to respect and love themselves. All this is possible when teachers focus on positive practices."

Healthy relationships prepare children for life and learning.

Making friends, playing well with others, and learning emotional self-control are essential to forming secure and satisfying relationships. We nurture social-emotional development by providing lots of time for children to play together and by modeling respectful communication. Without the sound foundation of a healthy emotional life and the ability to connect with others, it's difficult for children to flourish in any educational environment. Research from the National Academy of Sciences and others indicates that "Young children who develop strong early relationships with parents, family, caregivers, and teachers learn how to pay attention, cooperate, and get along with others. As a result, they are confident in their ability to explore and learn from the world around them."

A friend is someone who gives you total freedom to be yourself.

— *Jim Morrison*

Raising thoughtful citizens means proactively addressing diversity.

We want our children to be ready to sensitively engage with issues of gender, age, disability, race, religion, language, culture, and ethnicity. Therefore, we've adapted and incorporated Louise Derman-Sparks's goals for anti-bias curriculum:

— Fostering a knowledgeable, confident self-identity that doesn't need to feel superior to others.

— Nurturing intellectual and emotional dispositions and social skills that produce comfortable, empathetic interactions with people from diverse backgrounds.

— Encouraging critical thinking about bias, in which children recognize that unfair and untrue stereotypes, comments, and behaviors are hurtful to others.

— Developing the ability to stand up for oneself and others in the face of bias.

— Children model adult behavior, so we encourage parents to discuss diversity.

Diversity enhances creativity. It encourages the search for novel information and perspectives, leading to better decision making and problem solving.

— *Katherine W. Phillips*

Messy play builds brains.

Dress for mess is the official GPCDC clothing policy. And we're serious: One parent revealed that he regularly towels off excess mud before putting his daughter in the car. We have good reason for this policy. Young children are sensory creatures biologically wired to learn by taking action. Whether they are digging mud pits, playing in the dirt or sand, or finger-painting, sensory activities strengthen neural pathways and provide children with new information with which to make sense of their world.

Play that incorporates rich textural experiences allows children to express their emotions through manipulating the materials (clay, paint, sand) and refines their sense of touch. The richer the textural experiences, the richer their cognitive and language development will be ...

— *Liz Parnell*

We need creative thinkers if we want to solve the problems of the modern age.

Art education in early childhood develops a person's lifelong ability to think, perceive, and feel. Thoughtful art education can help children retain flexibility and confidence in their creative solutions. Yet, nationally, the arts are disappearing from education. Part of Patagonia's mission is "seeking creative solutions," so we've taken extra care to develop programs that have creativity at their core. Our center is infused with open-ended visual art, dance, music, storytelling, and theater.

It is important to develop creativity at a young age. It may be that the attitude of being creative—of finding the unknown challenging, coming up with many thoughts and ideas, looking for differences and similarities, having unique and original thoughts—is established early in life. At least it appears that these attitudes, once established, tend to be continuing.

— David Harrington, Jack Block, and Jeanne H. Block

We value teachers, because they raise those who will save the world.

Teachers have a profound impact on our children, families, and business. Appropriate child development is a science that involves intricate knowledge of children's developmental stages, how those stages fit together, and how that informs appropriate curricula. Good teachers make all of this happen effortlessly, which may explain why working with young children is undervalued and often described as "day care" or "babysitting." When educators aren't revered for their education, experience, and skill, parents and children, as well as the nation, lose.

Anything that can be done indoors can be done outdoors!

We joyfully fight the trend, observed by Professor Rhonda Clements, that 70 percent of women who said they played outdoors every day as kids reported that only 31 percent of their kids play outside daily. Playing outside ignites a world of learning that can't be duplicated indoors. So we fill our yards with nature: gardens, sand, mud, trees, and water. Children spend the bulk of their days outside, so all outdoor spaces accommodate every kind of play, as well as practical activities like napping and eating.

You are what you eat.

Food issues have long troubled us. Caring teachers and parents pay attention to the nutrition children need for their brain development. However, adults often include addictive sugary carbohydrate foods as treats for lunchtime, birthday parties, and holiday meals. We agree with food-policy expert Joan Dye Gussow that "Our uniquely American diets are rich in the wrong foods in bad proportions. Degenerative diseases take a long time to develop, but we know healthy eating equates to a healthy life." Today, technology and transportation put more distance between people and their food than ever. To counter this, we follow the Mayo Clinic's advice by serving fruit for dessert, offering water to drink, and avoiding empty calories from added sugars. Our twice-a-day snacks include organic, locally sourced fresh produce, ideally picked on-site. We serve food family-style, which can help kids scared of novelty to eat beyond their comfort zone and try foods with strong flavors or odd textures. Developing children's palates, a healthy relationship with food, and the social aspects of meals are priorities and equal to math, science, language arts, or any other discipline children are taught.

Predictable yet flexible routines build confidence and trust.

Children, whose lives are often dictated by adults' schedules, suffer more acutely when there aren't reliable plans that they can use to make sense of their day. Our program is designed around schedules predictable enough that children feel secure, but flexible enough to accommodate the needs of individuals. From signing in each morning with a parent to the rituals of eating lunch and napping, predictable routines help children feel stable and comfortable, so they can get down to the important work of growing up.

Home is not a place. Home is security, predictability, reliability, dependability, safety, permanence, combined together. — *Csaba Gabor-B*

Interactive electronic media are inappropriate for young children.

The closest our kids get to technology is playing telephone. The American Academy of Pediatrics recommends avoiding any screen time for children under the age of two and advocates limiting the use of media technology for all children because hours of screen time lead to attention problems, school difficulties, sleep and eating disorders, and obesity. To thrive, children need hands-on sensory play and lots of face-to-face interaction, so we provide environments that support friendship, direct experience, and building confidence.

Children who play in nature are happier and future champions for the environment.

As Richard Louv writes in his book *Last Child in the Woods,* children who play in nature are an endangered species. This is a serious problem because playing outside benefits kids in just about every way. Our kids spend much of their day outside in yards that we fill with as much wild nature as we can. They play in the mud, climb trees, tend gardens, and befriend local insects and animals. This allows them to form a personal relationship with nature that will benefit them for the rest of their lives.

Children should be taken to visit field, forest, hill, shore, the water, flowers, animals, the true homes of childhood. The very soul and body cry out for a more active, objective life, and to know nature firsthand.

— *Adapted from G. Stanley Hall*

An understanding heart is everything in a teacher ... One looks back with appreciation to the brilliant teachers, but with gratitude to those who touched our human feeling. The curriculum is so much necessary raw material, but warmth is the vital element for the growing plant and for the soul of the child.

— C. G. Jung

How do child-care programs create a culture of trust?

Chapter Three: Building Relationships

As our children grow up together, they raise one another through deep friendships founded on meaningful play. All of these bonds develop social-emotional skills: understanding and labeling feelings in self and others, working with strong emotions, peer interactions, and grounded confidence. Too often, schools focus exclusively on academics and sacrifice the time and skills needed to build social ties. The key to building children's strong relationships, with self and others, is positive connection—from birth—with caring adults. We hire gifted, well-trained professional caregivers who expertly weave connections between each other, parents, and children to create a nurturing community focused on raising children.

Consistency perpetuates bonding.

Our teacher turnover rate is extremely low. We do not outsource corporate-sponsored child care. It is on-site, an internal part of Patagonia, and our teachers enjoy the same benefits (401[k] matching, medical insurance, family leave, and on-site child care) offered to employees in all other divisions of the company. As a result, some staff members have been at GPCDC for three decades—the teacher shown here has been working with our children for 20 years. When teacher turnover rate is low, children reap the benefits of a stable, supportive community, which includes their current and former teachers. When GPCDC kids go off to kindergarten, it is not uncommon for teachers to visit them at their new schools.

With trust, children flourish.

On-site child care means all parents can see for themselves, at any time, that their children are receiving high-quality care. Parents communicate that sense of trust, consciously or unconsciously, to their children. Children who trust caregivers can thrive.

Students need to feel safe in order to take intellectual risks; they must be comfortable before they can venture into the realm of discomfort. Few things stifle creativity like the fear of being judged or humiliated. — *Alfie Kohn*

We welcome parents by being open and well-informed.

When prospective parents are researching centers, they should be offered a tour of the environment and have their questions thoughtfully answered. Different programs will have particular focuses; however, all good centers have the following:

— Low child-to-teacher ratios and small class sizes that allow children to explore, take risks, struggle with challenges, and take part in self-directed learning

— Educated teachers who continue to learn, participate in ongoing training, and have worked at the center for many years

— An experienced, enthusiastic, and well-educated director

— Basic accreditation—and beyond—plus good health and safety practices

— Ever-changing activities based on an understanding of child development

— Loving, positive relationships between teachers and children

Home visits establish relationships before the first day.

Each child (up to age three) has a specially assigned teacher who is that child's one-on-one caregiver. The primary caregiver meets the child for the first time by visiting him or her at home. During the home visit, the caregiver begins bonding with the child (and vice versa) and exchanges information with the parents. The home visit acts as a bridge between the familiarity of home and the initial unfamiliarity of the center.

A child's first days at GPCDC require a loving transition.

Before a child officially starts the program, parents are required to spend 10 hours with their child in the center to learn routines and help the child acclimate and establish trust. During the first week, primary caregivers spend one-on-one time with the new child and become attuned to the child's emotional needs. For example, pacifiers are typically used only at nap time, but during the first day at GPCDC, some infants need pacifiers.

Saying good-bye can be difficult.

Caregivers understand that it can be hard for adults and children to say good-bye. They coach parents to keep departures short, to exude confidence and resolve as they exit, and refrain from sneaking out or asking the child for permission to leave.

With time, as infants internalize their new routines, they learn to trust that their parents will return.

— *Nicole Marie*

Trust is maintained by ongoing communication.

Frequent communication maintains and deepens trust. With parents on-site, teachers can often share stories and information daily. We also have quarterly classroom meetings and parent-teacher conferences. For parents of infants, conferences are every two months; for parents of two-year-olds, every three months; and conferences for the parents of preschoolers are every six months. These include developmental assessments, anecdotes illustrating the child's developmental level, and videos to show how the child interacts and behaves with the other children and staff.

— GPCDC Practice —

Changing classrooms is done with care.

Change can be difficult—even for adults who have had years of experience with all sorts of change. We understand that young children cope differently, and, for some, change is stressful. Like all quality schools, we plan for transitions thoughtfully and carefully. Caregivers and parents meet to discuss the transition process, and then caregivers create a two-week-long transition plan, during which the child spends more and more time in the new room. One month before the transition, the child visits the new classroom with the original primary caregiver, and the new caregiver also visits the child in his or her present classroom. Throughout the transition, the original caregiver accompanies the child to the new room and remains on the sidelines to give the child and new caregiver time and space to bond. Caregivers carefully observe the child and when the child seems comfortable, the former caregiver leaves, but remains on-call to offer support. If the child has not acclimated to the new classroom after the two-week period (a rare occurrence), both the former and new caregiver meet and create a revised strategy.

When parents can stop by anytime, everyone benefits.

From 9 a.m. to 5 p.m., five days a week, most working parents don't see their children. On-site child care means that moms and dads can share time with their kids in the middle of the workday, between meetings, or during lunch. In these photos, Patagonia employees visit with their children at the center, in our design studio, and on the play yard. Research demonstrates that children do better academically and socially when parents are involved, so child-care centers benefit by welcoming them. An open-door policy assures mothers and fathers that a center has nothing to hide. A worried parent can quickly stop by and see his or her child joyfully playing and then return to work with confidence. This increases employees' productivity and fosters loyalty to the company, which is good for business.

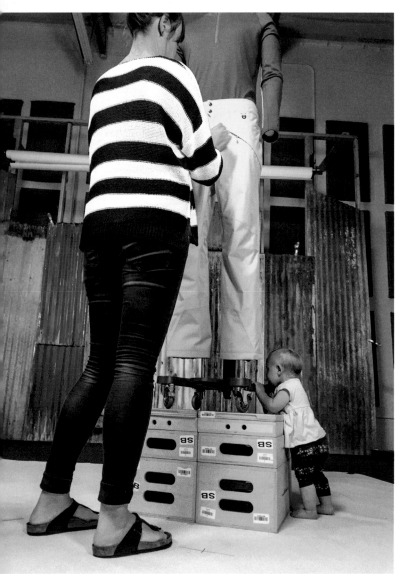

Kids are welcome to visit their parents at work.

When children visit their parents in the workplace, the value of work is modeled for them, and from a very young age, they come to understand what their parents do all day. Children also transform the office with vitality and whimsy, reminding us that first and foremost we are human.

When your child physically knows your work, your child is psychologically part of your work. — *Jennifer Ridgeway*

Children's friendships are an essential part of the curriculum.

After children feel secure in their attachments to adults, they branch out to form relationships with one another. Children's friendships impact the social and emotional development of the individual child. Because our program begins in infancy and ends in elementary school, children develop relationships over many years. Rough-and-tumble play is a normal part of the child's bonding process. We know it's working when we see smiles.

Infants and toddlers socialize through direct contact.

Infants crawl all over other babies and adults. It's usually not a problem, but we watch children's bodies and facial expressions. If one child displays stress, we move the infants apart. **Teachers say:** "Sam, you look like you were trying to move away from Christopher's hugs. Christopher, I am picking you up and moving you over. Sam is trying to tell you he doesn't want any more hugs." Teachers remind children to be "*suave*/gentle," and also that "hands are not for hitting." We teach infants to sign "play" and "stop," so they can communicate nonverbally.

Stop

— *Parent Story* —

The Red Snapper

Years ago, one of the kids, a redhead who was not yet walking, started crawling up to other babies and biting them. When he did this, the caregiver would pick him up and hold him while she called his mother. The mother was then required to take him home for the day. Eventually, he was biting so frequently that he was sent home with his mother for a month. Before he could officially re-enter the program, we required that a child psychologist evaluate the boy for a full day as he interacted with his class. On the child's first day back, the biting behavior commenced immediately. The psychologist watched. And then she said, "Have you noticed that he gets exactly what he wants when he bites? Try removing him from the situation, not having his mother come to him, and not sending him home." The biting stopped right away. GPCDC now has a five-page policy on how to handle biting.

Lesson learned: To prevent our two-year-olds from biting each other, we provide teething pacifiers, also called teethers. One hot day, a teacher gave frozen teethers to several young children who were playing on the mixed-age playground. Within minutes, the older children requested teethers, arguing that they would keep them from biting other children. We didn't have 50 teethers, but we promised to get more—and we made it a teaching moment. We talked to the older children about the difference between their abilities to control their impulses and to resolve conflicts compared to younger children. We also discussed our expectations for older versus younger children. Thanks to overnight shipping, we had teethers for everyone within two days.

Transcend traditional discipline—consider the root of challenging behaviors.

Traditional discipline curbs symptoms, while community-minded practice helps children find social worth. To avoid the need for discipline, teachers set up spaces that meet kids' needs. But teachers also maintain boundaries and remind children, for example, that they may not throw blocks. But they don't stop there. If a child repeatedly knocks over others' buildings, instead of creating a rule, *No one can knock over buildings*, teachers consider why behaviors happen: *Is the child trying to play?* **Teachers say:** "Do you want to help Alana build? Perhaps you can add blocks with her?" Consider altering the environment, as shown in the photos. For example, if the child is interested in deconstruction, set up materials to explore it.

Children are inherently kind.

Anyone who has witnessed a two-year-old's tantrum can attest that young children's conflicts are loud. Tantrums aside, most interactions between children are successful. Observe a playground, and you'll see more moments of harmony than conflict. In the photos above, a toddler wants to be gentle but lacks the requisite motor skills. Contrast that to the older child who comforts a friend he accidentally hit with a soccer ball. Psychologist Martin Hoffman reports that "The evidence increasingly points to an innate disposition [in children] to be responsive to the plight of other people ... Creating people who are socially responsive does not totally depend on parents and teachers. Such socializing agents have an ally within the child."

Conflict is a valuable part of community.

Conflict is unavoidable and essential because it allows us to learn about our desires and discover different perspectives. Children experience conflict as just another part of life. They often gravitate toward a conflict that they are not involved in because they want to study what's happening or offer suggestions. Teachers can channel children's natural curiosity to forge solutions to disputes.

"I need space!"

Helping children communicate their emotions is often a challenge. We remind children to ask for help verbally or by using sign language, and then teachers respond accordingly. When conflicts arise, we don't use meaningless phrases, such as "Play nicely" or "Say you're sorry." We help children verbalize feelings and desires to understand the underlying causes of conflict. **Teachers say:** "I hear you asking for help. Would you like me to help your friend to the other side of the swing set?" or "I saw you yelling at each other. I saw you hit George. You may not hit him. Are you okay, George?" Caregivers always take the time to comfort the injured child before exploring the root of the conflict, such as "Was there something you were trying to tell George? You need space? Your friend needs space too."

Conflicts are about property disputes.

No environment is more communal than preschool classrooms where children negotiate the use of almost every object. Communal environments can be challenging, but they give children the opportunity to learn to wait, to communicate their wants, and to empathize. When sharing conflicts occur, children need to hear more than "Remember to share." Sharing refers to a complex set of norms that adults use to deal politely with ownership. For children, the word *sharing* is vague and not useful. Instead, we model phrases that defuse conflicts. **Teachers say:** "Hector was using that ball when you grabbed it, Luke. Hector, what's your plan for that ball? Luke, what was your plan? Can you use it together? No? Luke, you can use it when Hector is finished, or I'll help you find another ball."

Teachers don't guide play, they facilitate it. When there is a problem, they ask open-ended questions or articulate observations, which usually prompts kids to find solutions themselves. Telling children how to resolve a problem robs them of their "aha" moment.

— *Nicole Marie*

Every community grapples with inclusion and exclusion.

Inclusion and exclusion are a source of conflict in preschool. Children grapple with it: "I just want to play with John!" Parents grapple with it, too: "Should I invite everyone to the birthday party?" There isn't one method for ensuring that no one feels left out. Schools must consider positions on the following questions: Do children have the right to spend time one-on-one with each other? How do our personal histories with exclusion affect the way we react? What values are important to us, and how does exclusion relate to those? Are there practices and policies that implicitly communicate values about inclusion and exclusion?

What to say when children don't want to play:

We don't require our children to play with everyone, but teachers help children by offering empathetic, polite language to use when they decline offers to play with others. **Teachers say:** "Thank you for asking. Could we play another time?" We also remind children who don't want to play with others to remember how it feels to be left out. The excluded child is invited to join another activity or group. When a child is excluded, there is the opportunity to say, "Do you remember when you wouldn't play with Elena?"

Conflicts are an excellent source of curriculum.

When children continually fight about something, teachers ask the group for help. Children are often more aware of social nuances than teachers. Plus, if children provide solutions, they are more likely to adhere to them. Solving problems also requires children to synthesize their thoughts, consider others' solutions, and compromise.

If the children's resolutions are outlandish or impractical, try them nevertheless. Should the solutions fail, begin the conversation again—this process truly empowers children at school. Keep in mind that young children are still learning to articulate their needs and to control their impulses, so some conflicts will end in tears.

Emotional intelligence is built by relating.

When children struggle with the complexities of friendship and are wisely guided through conflict, they develop emotional intelligence along the way. Healthy relationships hinge on these emotional skills:

— Identifying and labeling one's feelings
— Recognizing emotions in others
— Responding appropriately to emotions

Talking about emotions is crucial—especially with boys.

Research indicates that adults tend to talk about emotions more often with girls than with boys. When this happens, boys have a hard time coping with others' emotions and their own. Careful adults do not let unconscious bias stunt any child's emotional growth. Teachers can use social interactions to build emotional skills.

Teachers do and say:
— Point out physical indicators of emotion: "I saw that you got angry and started to cry when he took the tricycle."
— Label the emotion: "It looks like you are angry."
— Suggest an appropriate course of action: "I wonder if you want to talk to him about your plans for riding the tricycle?"

Children use free play to integrate challenging emotions.

As one listens to children playing, one sometimes hears things such as "Let's pretend Daddy died"; "I can't play now, I'm too busy with my baby"; or "I won't let you steal my house!" When teachers carefully observe children at play, they learn about children's feelings and can use that information to provide emotional support. As brain scientist Oliver Sacks noted, "Very young children love and demand stories, and can understand complex matters presented as stories, when their powers of comprehending general concepts, paradigms, are almost non-existent." For example, weapon play is about power, a central theme to childhood. It's often part of a story, which teachers let play out, as long as children aren't hurting one another. In the photo above, children play with "light sabers" they've crafted from paper.

Building grounded confidence.

Psychologists once hailed self-esteem as the measure of a healthy emotional life, and a generation of children was rewarded for anything and everything (think of the ubiquitous trophy for sports participation), whether rewards were warranted or not. Today, psychologists know that disingenuous praise causes children to mistrust adults, shields kids from disappointment, and breeds a lack of resilience. What's needed is a shift toward grounded confidence based on hard work, actual achievement, honesty, and self-reflection.

Insecurity can provide a moment for self-reflection.

When a child says, "I'm not good at gymnastics," and they're right, we must resist saying, "Oh no, you're great, honey." Children know it's not true, and we send the message that admitting weakness is not allowed. They also don't get the help they're asking for. We opt for better responses. **Teachers say:** "It can be hard when you can't do what you want. What do you want to get better at? Would you like help getting better?" Caring teachers know when to offer support and when to step back. It's important to let children struggle, because it's through toil that children gain self-motivation and self-reliance, as well as a sense of their limits.

Resilience is developed by praising hard work.

When we focus on hard work, children develop a growth mind-set, a belief that hard work pays off. **Teachers say:** "You worked on that puzzle day after day and finally got it! I can see you've really been trying hard." Whereas, overly praising for things that come easily, "Look how fast you did that puzzle. You are so smart," creates a fixed mind-set. The belief that one is inherently smart or not can cause children to shy away from challenges.

If success means they are smart then failure means they are dumb, that's the fixed mind-set.

— *Carol Dweck*

Children benefit from relationships with the larger society.

When we take walks into neighborhoods around GPCDC, we encounter police officers, doctors, shopkeepers, pet owners, and surfers. Children are naturally curious about the people they meet in the world—much of their play revolves around community roles. Teachers can encourage children to see themselves as part of their larger society by building relationships between children and the world at large.

Raising empowered citizens will change the world.

In school, children learn to be citizens. As we face climate change, disparities between rich and poor, and complicated questions about ever-more-powerful technology, we need citizens who care about community and can speak difficult truths.

On the International Day of Peace, I urge you to join us in our celebrations and in making resolutions for each of us to do our part in working toward environmental sustainability. ... We cannot achieve the United Nations' Sustainable Development Goals unless we work together to make this a better world for people, other animals, and the environment.

— *Jane Goodall*

How do child-care routines communicate values to children?

Chapter Four: Intentional Routines

Children experience time not in minutes and hours, but as a series of events, and they use routines to predict what's coming next. Routines help children relax; they don't have to worry about how or when something will happen. When it comes to practices like eating, napping, and diapering, activities that children traditionally resist, routines are invaluable. Clear expectations and predictable sequences reduce power struggles and transform the mundane elements of life into meaningful rituals. Every good routine also incorporates elements of flexibility because no matter how much we plan, life is unpredictable. Intentional routines are a powerful way to communicate values to children, so they need to be constructed in ways that respect children's autonomy and empower them to become masters of self-care.

"We not only respect [children] ... we demonstrate our respect every time we interact with them. Respecting a child means treating even the youngest infant as a unique human being, not as an object." *— Magda Gerber*

Off to a good start: the morning routine.

Routines communicate our values to children. GPCDC's morning schedule tells parents and children that we understand it's a big deal to transition from home to the center. Ideally, mornings start slowly, giving parents and children time together in the classroom. Parents and children naturally develop their routines. They might read two books together before the good-bye, play a game of chase outside, or share an organic breakfast at our on-site café. GPCDC opens at 7:30 a.m., but families are welcome to drop off children anytime after that. We find that the transition from home to school is easier if families are able to do it at their own pace.

GPCDC closes at 5:15 p.m., so families have time together.

We want families to have time in the evening for walks, meals, and bedtime stories. Although on-site child care can ease the demands of work versus family, there is no substitute for time together at home.

Children and parents build meaningful departure routines—saying good-bye to teachers and friends, having one last swing on the play yard or biking home—before they enjoy their end-of-day rituals.

On-site care enhances bonding between parents and infants.

Nursing is the first routine that mothers and infants establish. Returning to work can be stressful because moms and babies must disrupt what they worked hard to accomplish. On-site care allows mothers to preserve nursing rituals. They don't spend money and time on cumbersome machines. They don't have the burden of finding a place to pump at work. Instead, nursing mothers are encouraged and accommodated. For bottle-fed babies, we support bonding by asking parents to give children their bottles (caregivers step in if a parent can't). Infants determine when they want to eat, and we accommodate their needs by providing areas where parents can feed babies uninterrupted.

Meals are meaningful routines and the foundation of community.

During school meals, children learn to dine communally, sharing stories and responsibilities. They also master self-help skills and develop confidence and independence. Whether children are learning to grasp a spoon or open a tricky container, we use mealtimes to encourage them to hone their skills. Child-size chairs are available, and children use them when they're ready. We don't use highchairs or place children in chairs; instead, teachers coach children who are learning to get into chairs. **Caregivers say:** "Your knee is on the seat. It looks like you're trying to turn. How will you do that? You turned a bit; now your foot is stuck. You look frustrated, but you're working hard. You've turned, and now you're seated."

Toddlers develop resilience by eating independently.

By the time our children crawl up into a chair at the snack table, they're getting the hang of feeding themselves, so we introduce new skills, such as pouring water. Teachers advise putting as much water in the pitcher as you're willing to clean up. No matter how many times children spill, we still let them fill their own water glasses. A little spilled water is worth the focus, mastery, tenacity, and resilience successful pouring provides our children.

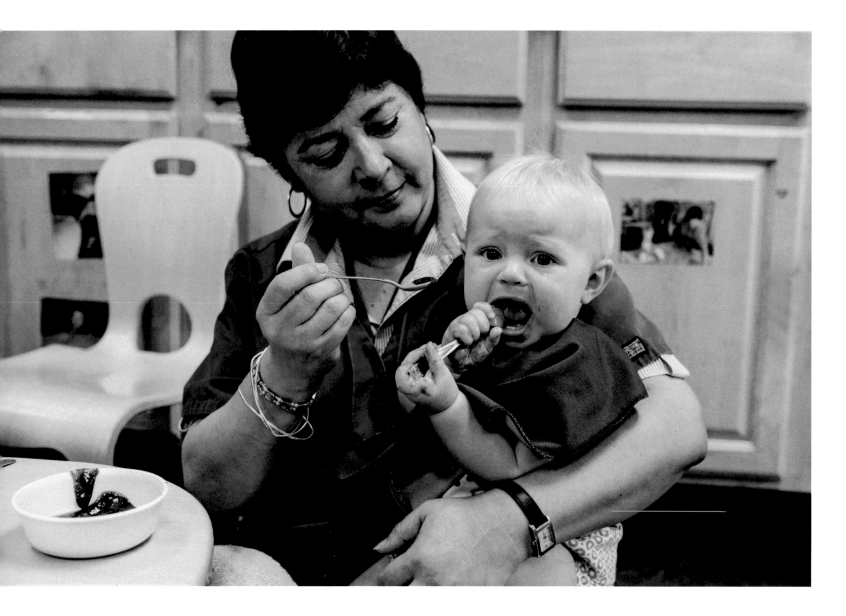

Infants are capable and independent—if given opportunities.

The infant classroom at mealtime demonstrates that, given the opportunity, even young children are very capable. Infants sit in a caregiver's lap for meals. Whether infants can feed themselves or not, they are offered utensils to hold. Eating is self-initiated, and infants create their own schedules. There's much to talk about during meals, and we've found that narrating and sign language can help infants communicate. **Caregivers say:** "The applesauce you are eating has a grainy texture, and the yogurt is smoother and creamier. You're scooping from the bowl with your spoon. I see your bowl is empty, and you are trying to reach the serving bowl with your spoon. Are you asking for more? It feels like you are trying to get off of my lap, are you telling me you are done?"

Caregiving practices with choices foster autonomy.

During meals, children are in control, and caregivers offer choices. Children choose a seat, a bib, a bowl, a spoon, whether to eat inside or outside, and what and how much to eat. **Caregivers say:** "Do you want the blue or red bib? Which spoon would you like?" Children practice opening containers independently. This takes some effort, and children can get frustrated when it's lunchtime and they're hungry. Caregivers stay calm, and help as needed. For safety, we have two important mealtime rules: To avoid allergic reactions, children may not eat others' food; and children must sit while eating to avoid choking.

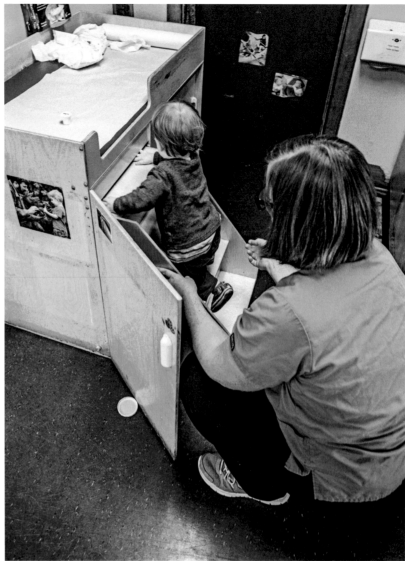

Diaper changes can—and should—empower children.

Respectful and consistent caregiving practices show children that caregivers have their best interests at heart. When diapering and dressing babies and toddlers, we use the RIE methodology, because we believe that these practices empower children. Providing kids with choices gives them flexibility when they don't want a diaper change. **Caregivers say:** "Changing your diaper isn't a choice. But you can choose how to get to the table: Do you want to crawl like a cat or hop like a bunny?" Our caregivers are accommodating problem-solvers and do things with and for our children—not to them. For example, in the photos above, the child opens the diapering table door, climbs, and chooses his diaper. He climbs down and washes his hands with just enough help to be successful.

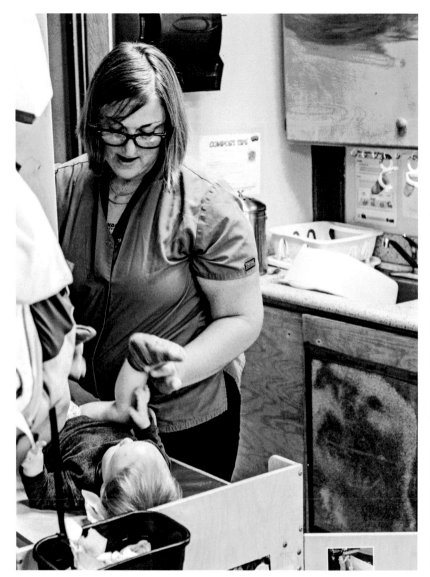

When it's time for a diaper change, caregivers say:

"I'm getting the table ready. When I come back, it's time to change your diaper." She then says and signs, "My gloves are on; the table is ready. It's time." Depending on the child's age, teachers pick up or walk the child to the table and always inform them before doing anything: "I'm going to pick you up now. I'm laying you down.

I'm going to take your pants and diaper off. The wipes will be cold. All done. Which diaper do you want? Can you help put your leg in the pants? We need to use soap when we wash our hands. Can you get a towel? Let's pat, pat, pat those hands dry."

Caregivers help babies get themselves to sleep.

When it comes to sleeping, our goal is for children to self-soothe and fall asleep on their own, but getting there is a process. Younger children sleep in cribs then transition to mats as toddlers. Those who sleep on mats may choose to sleep inside or out. We observe and narrate infants' cues. **Caregivers say:** "When you rub your eyes and cry, you're telling me you're tired. In two minutes, we'll walk to your crib so you can rest." We might help infants relax by holding them if that's their routine at home, and if they are accustomed to pacifiers, we allow them. Children are taught to say "sleepy" and "read books" in English, Spanish, and sign language. Eventually, children shed aids and caregivers adapt, gently supporting and guiding them toward independent self-soothing.

Nap time practices can build competence and autonomy.

Even young children can set up their mats and bedding, then put them away after nap time. When the two-year-olds get ready to nap, they retrieve and place their sheet on their mat and choose a book to read.

They may chat with friends or get a drink of water before settling down to sleep. We also recognize that they are still young and might require a back rub or a book read aloud by a teacher to fall asleep.

Dressing builds self-reliance and responsibility.

Clothing is a form of creative expression.

Even very young infants will choose between two outfits presented to them by looking at one longer than the other. Teachers encourage children to decide whether they need a jacket or want to wear shorts on a hot day and intervene only if safety is concerned. Children may choose to go barefoot or wear shoes.

The benefits of going barefoot include improved body awareness, leg strength, and agility. Being barefoot also benefits the brain. According to pediatric specialist Dr. Kacie Flegal, if babies are barefoot, " ... the little pads of babies' feet feel, move, and balance on the surface that they are exploring, the information sent to the brain from tactile, proprioceptive, and vestibular pathways quiet, or inhibit, other extraneous sensory input. This creates focus and awareness of walking and moving through space; babies get more tuned in to their surroundings."

Play gives children a chance to practice what they are learning.

— *Fred Rogers*

— *Parent Story* —

Choices

I have to admit that being an art and design major, my knowledge of child development comes from babysitting here and there as a teenager and skimming *What to Expect When You're Expecting*. I have been figuring it out as I go, with tremendous help from the GPCDC teachers, who have given insight to the complexities of my infant, now toddler. Though I do my best to keep discipline consistent at home, it was pretty difficult one particularly trying day of work and parenting to keep a straight face when talking to my 18-month-old. I was rushing him out the classroom door without giving him a choice. "It's time to go home," I said and grabbed his chubby little hand. I reached for the doorknob, and he stopped in his tracks. I looked down at his round face, his eyes squinted up at me, and he said, "Or?"

Lesson learned: In this scenario, I could have offered the choices of hopping, skipping, or somersaulting to the car.

On the move.

When younger children need to get around the Patagonia campus or go on a field trip, they use specially built wagons or a walking rope. Since the fateful day back in 1984 when a parent accidentally left his child at school, GPCDC has offered after-school pickup at local elementary schools for children in kindergarten through third grade. During the drive from school to GPCDC, teachers and children talk about the school day and the afternoon ahead. After the busy school day, children often call their parents when they arrive at Kids' Club.

Routines for illness, safety, and emergencies prepare everyone.

Fires, earthquakes, fevers, and scrapes—we're prepared for it all. When children fall, the sign "hurt" is used to indicate the injury, and the sign "help" means the child wants assistance. **Teachers say:** "We're going to put ice on your knee. I want to help you. It's cold, you can touch it. Here we go." During fire drills, teachers place babies in wheeled cribs and talk about "going for a walk" together. We have an illness policy in place, which includes administering informal health checks every day. When children become hurt or sick, parents are notified immediately, and we document the incident. Children go home if necessary.

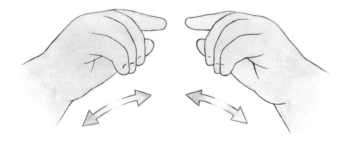

Hurt

Why is unstructured play crucial?

Chapter Five: Creative Play

Unstructured play, where children get messy and wild, where the unpredictability of nature is available to surprise and delight, is the pinnacle of play. In a world that often expects children to put aside "childish ways" in favor of "preparing" for the future, we stand for the right of children to play, because we know that play is how children prepare for the future. We are not alone in this belief. Experts of all stripes have stated that play is an essential part of a healthy childhood. According to pediatric occupational therapist Angela Hanscom, if children don't get enough unstructured playtime, "They are more likely to be clumsy, have difficulty paying attention, trouble controlling their emotions, utilize poor problem-solving methods, and demonstrate difficulties with social interactions."

"The very existence of youth is due in part to the necessity for play; the animal does not play because he is young, he has a period of youth because he must play." — *Karl Groos*

What is play?

Although play is easy to identify, it turns out that defining play is actually difficult. Many researchers have labeled different kinds of play and characterized what qualities constitute play. Here are a few elements that we believe are part of good play: Play is fun. Children do it for the satisfaction of playing. Even if children have a goal, such as "Let's climb to the top of the tree," the journey is more important than the destination. Children freely choose to play and are actively engaged, whether physically, verbally, or through observation. Finally, play is imaginative and doesn't need to reflect reality.

Children need to spend a large portion of their day outdoors to get the stimulation and natural learning experiences they are born to crave. We believe that hands-on experiential learning is the best educational approach for children. Being outdoors provides them with not only fresh air, it encourages imaginative play, creativity, hand-eye coordination, balance, physical strength, and mental clarity. — *Field & Forest Outdoor Preschool*

When children play, the teacher's role is to step back and observe.

Play flourishes when adults support it in a skillful and subtle manner. If adults are too involved and directive, play deteriorates. Our children direct their own play. Teachers support play by setting up environments that reflect kids' interests. When conflict arises or children have difficulty starting to play, they support them in a variety of ways. For the most part, teachers act as mentoring guides; they observe as the rich world of children's play unfolds.

What to say when supporting play

Teachers respond to play—when invited to do so—with open-ended questions, augmenting the learning that's already taking place.

In order to promote thinking, they ask:
"I wonder what will happen if you add red to yellow paint?"

"What do you think will happen if you put another shell on this side of the scale?"

To prompt an evaluation of feelings, they ask:
"How would you feel if Nick took a paintbrush from you while you were using it?"

"How did it make you feel when you and Tommy built the tower together?"

To encourage problem solving, they ask:
"Why do you think the block keeps sliding off the top?"

"How could you stop yourself from falling off the scooter?"

To encourage reflection or evaluation, they ask:
"How do you feel about what you did?"

"What would you do next time?"

What to say when there's a conflict. Teachers follow these steps when negotiating a conflict during play:

1. Each child talks about the problem:
"So, what's the problem? We've heard Liam, now let's hear from Thomas."

2. The adult reiterates the problem:
"Liam wants to move these ramps we built for our cars near the tree. Thomas doesn't because he's worried the ramps will come apart if we move them there. What can we do?"

3. The children suggest solutions:
"Liam says we should get two different ramps for the cars and put them under the tree."

4. Adults use questions to help kids pick a solution:
"Why will this idea solve the problem? How do you think your friend will feel? Does everyone agree to doing it this way?"
"Thomas, what do you think? You agree? How can we help Liam get the two ramps to the tree?"

5. Give the solution a try! If it's not working, help the kids come up with another solution.

6. When they arrive at a working resolution, validate their problem-solving, empathy, and communication skills.
"How did that work? It looks like you reached a solution that works for both of you."

The foundation of play is exploration.

Whether kids are climbing trees, hunting for bugs, or pretending to fly to the moon, exploration is central to play. Infants play by exploring their hands, fingers, and toes. Toddlers leave no stone unturned. All kids use play to investigate their senses and delve into relationships. Children are inherent explorers—curious about the unfamiliar and interested in challenges. We strive to keep them that way.

Our teachers have an eye for simple items that can be transformed into experiences, plus we have a sewing room, design studio, café, and retail store—all of which can serve as sources for reusable raw materials, including fabric remnants, cardboard boxes, and long tubes from fabric bolts. Children's interests unfold best in their play when they are fashioning toys out of found objects, rather than commercial toys.

Wild play develops imagination and creativity.

Most of us spent our childhoods being told "Go outside and play." Once outside, we used our imagination and creativity to figure out what to do. Children today, entertained by electronics, are staying indoors. To combat this trend, we look to the adventure playground movement, founded 80 years ago by a Danish architect. Adventure playgrounds are stocked with wood, loose parts, and tools. Risk, ingenuity, and independence abound as kids build their own equipment. In our play yards, we combine loose parts and tools with natural landscapes and a respect for kids' independence to create a place where children can go truly wild. This wild play has an important role in all areas of development. Many believe that playing outside has a positive impact on manual dexterity, depth perception, physical coordination and tactile sensitivity.

Constructive play is rich with thought and inventiveness.

Carl Jung astutely observed that "The creation of something new is not accomplished by the intellect but by the play." Constructive play is a rich form of play because it engages children's minds, hands, and imaginations. To build something new and different, kids must think mathematically, then create stories about what they're building, and negotiate particulars with others. There are physical challenges as children balance pieces or place tiny details. Teachers just need to provide compelling materials—children will not only build fantastic structures but also life skills.

A child loves his play, not because it's easy, but because it's hard. *— Benjamin Spock*

Play can be challenging.

When did you last recruit friends and entice them to play a role in a game complex enough to be interesting but simple enough to follow? Sound easy? It's not. Play is difficult. Objects are unruly. Everyone wants things to go their way. What you imagine is often impossible to achieve. Sometimes frustration motivates kids to solve problems. Other times, it can be too much. By learning children's cues, teachers know when to provide minimal support that still allows children to experience self-reliance while achieving their goals.

Teachers also keep in mind that when children play games where everything goes according to plan, they quickly drift away. The goal of play isn't racing to the finish but relishing the journey. We are inspired by the adventure playground movement, which encourages providing children with tools and a plethora of building materials so they can create their own challenges. In the photo above, left, GPCDC kids use tools to fill sandbags for an incoming El Niño storm; and on the right, children invent their own way to climb using materials at hand.

The value of unstructured play.

The value of unstructured play is best summarized by filmmaker Erin Davis, who recently completed a documentary called *The Land*, which is about an adventure playground in North Wales. "Kids now are the same as they ever were, and have been throughout time. They climb things, they hide in things, they create dens and places to hide in, create hierarchies and worlds of their own. They're drawn to fire; they're super-imaginative. What's different [today] is the degree to which they have an opportunity to express and pursue these interests. So it's surprising to us—but really it shouldn't be—that kids thrive in these environments when they can do really whatever they want. They have the play drive. It's up to us to provide the kinds of opportunities for them to really follow through on it."

Only the outdoors can provide the variety and stimulation of all the developing senses. Children initiating their own curiosity to explore and discover provides a personal relationship with their own feelings of competence in the natural world. Outdoors fosters resilient, independent, creative learners. The young explorer is stimulated with the "... ever-changing moods and marvels, potential and challenges of the natural world through the seasons."

— *Ethos and Principles of Forest Schools*

Stages of play range from solitary to cooperative.

We give children uninterrupted time to explore and choose what and where to play. We also respect the stages of play: solitary, parallel, associative, and cooperative. The photos above illustrate solitary play, in which children play alone. Parallel play, shown on the facing page, is marked by children doing similar activities without referring to one another. Although all children use every stage of play, infants and babies tend to spend more time in solitary play and progress toward social play as they get older.

Types of social play: associative and cooperative.

Many factors, ranging from communication skills to how well children know each other, influence whether children play alone or with others. When children play separately yet are influenced by and reference each other, it is called associative play. In the photo to the left, the boys play in the same space and chat back and forth about what each is doing, but they lack a shared goal. The situation shown above is different: These children engage in cooperative play and have a common goal. Cooperative play is evidenced by behaviors such as interacting by sharing objects or speaking to one another, creating collective goals and story lines and working together to achieve them.

Physical play is body centered: running, jumping, and climbing.

While physicality is always part of play, the term "physical play" is defined by body-centric play. It's rolling, running, jumping, chasing, and leaping for the sake of movement itself. According to a research summary by the Minnesota Children's Museum, "Despite the potential physical and cognitive benefits bestowed by physical activity, physical play is one of the least researched forms of play. It is also one of the most endangered forms of play in our schools and society: Recess in schools is disappearing at an alarming rate, and active play among youngsters has plummeted by 50 percent over the last 40 years."

There is a difference between danger and risk. Our environments reflect this difference by being free of hazards but full of challenges. Teachers are available to support children but ultimately want kids to accurately assess risks themselves. — *Nicole Marie*

Imagination fuels play.

Making up games starts with an imaginative idea, some conversation, and a plan. These two children laid out a course of action, implemented their idea through trial and error, then successfully stood together on their bridge.

Movement play lights up the brain and fosters learning, innovation, flexibility, adaptability, and resilience. These central aspects of human nature require movement to be fully realized.

— *Stuart Brown, MD, and Christopher Vaughan*

Object play is an early form of play that lasts a lifetime.

As soon as infants learn to reach and grasp, they begin to play with objects. It's one of the first kinds of play that develops in infants, and many adults still enjoy a solitary puzzle or game of ball. Object play happens when items are playfully manipulated, and it is embedded in all kinds of play. Stacking rocks, throwing a ball, or twirling a piece of fabric, the world is always calling to be arranged and rearranged.

It is easy to overlook the quieter forms of object play because they can be unobtrusive and solitary. However, the child tinkering away in the corner is developing important knowledge about the nature of the physical world. Teachers set up interesting and inviting areas, then stand back and watch children explore. Kids often use materials and spaces in ways teachers never imagined.

The child amidst his baubles is learning
the action of light, motion, gravity, [and]
muscular force ... — *Ralph Waldo Emerson*

Social play helps build community.

While all children, even babies, play with others, social play becomes a priority in the preschool years. But it's not only the way children develop social skills; it's the way they build community. Our teachers encourage pro-social behaviors, including empathy, cooperation, and helpfulness in group play. For children, playing together is intimate and sacred, and it's the time when they reveal their innermost thoughts and feelings.

Play, while it cannot change the external realities of children's lives, can be a vehicle for children to explore and enjoy their differences and similarities and to create, even for a brief time, a more just world where everyone is an equal and valued participant. — *Patricia G. Ramsey*

Pretend play peaks in preschool and starts to wane in middle childhood.

Children who are about a year old will use their bodies to pretend to do things like sleep and eat. Two-year-olds will transform objects—a banana becomes a telephone, and a ball turns into an apple. Eventually, children use fewer props and are able to be more abstract so that all the world becomes a stage. When kids play firefighters, mothers, and butterflies, they process life and take on new identities. The child afraid of monsters becomes a superhero to save her friends from evil, feeling courageous and reassured that she has power over her fears. The day she decides to be the monster, she discovers we all have a little monster inside and by embodying it, the monsters outside aren't quite as scary.

Children forge their own reality in fantasy play.

In *The Boy Who Would Be a Helicopter*, Vivian Gussin Paley observes that "'Pretend' often confuses the adult, but it is the child's real and serious world, the stage upon which any identity is possible and secret thoughts can be safely revealed." In fantasy play, children both re-create reality and construct imagined worlds. Teachers supply the materials for both. Kids get uninterrupted time to build play scripts and act out their ideas. Sometimes teachers label emotions expressed, ask exploratory questions, and offer materials to expand pretend play.

Imagination is more important than knowledge. For knowledge is limited to all we now know and understand, while imagination embraces the entire world, and all there ever will be to know and understand.

— *Albert Einstein*

Kids imitate what adults say and do.

For better or worse, imitation is how culture is transmitted. Children use play as a form of imitation, as the photos on these pages demonstrate. For example, when children have a new sibling in the family, playing out domestic rituals from home can help them process the change. Pretending to cook and clean are favorite games among two- and three-year-olds and speaks to their desire to be independent, industrious, and model adults' behaviors. Through close observation of play, we can track how children are interpreting what adults do. As a result, our teachers use the same language with each other that they teach children. Teachers also play with an attitude of wonder and awe. They honor agreements, eat healthy foods, and compost leftovers. Children will always find unrefined bits of adult behavior and reflect them back, often through play. When they do, we do our best to improve our conduct. If we want to change culture by influencing the next generation, we've got to, as they say, be the change we want to see.

Play is joyful.

Given all of the benefits and intricacies of play, it can be easy to forget that at its core, play is a source of joy. We never want to lose sight of the fact that play is fundamentally joyful. Teachers and children share joyful moments, and teachers identify the emotions: "I see you smiling as you and Anna ride that scooter." Children have always played, and despite being overscheduled and inundated with technology, they continue to do so. Play brings meaning to kids' lives. It connects them to friends, family, animals, places, and ideas. It's the way they discover and create themselves. Protecting play—wild, imaginative, creative play—is an important responsibility that we take on wholeheartedly.

Play energizes us and enlivens us. It eases our burdens. It renews our natural sense of optimism and opens us up to new possibilities.

— *Stuart Brown, MD*

How can environments inspire children?

Chapter Six: Exploring Indoors and Outdoors

Classroom environments—both inside and out—are another kind of teacher.
When classrooms are beautiful and inviting, families feel valued and welcome.
When materials are accessible, interesting, and well-organized, children are encouraged to think and relate. Thoughtful environments don't happen by accident.
They're the product of deliberate intention and ongoing evaluation. While setting up spaces, teachers ask themselves, "What are the goals for this space? Is the space appealing, safe, and appropriately equipped for the age ranges?" It's important to step back and assess all environments, because we want to provide a comfortable, creative, and dynamic home away from home.

"We may say that the adult works to perfect his environment, whereas the child works to perfect himself, using the environment as the means." *— Maria Montessori*

Our infant rooms accommodate babies' needs for activity and quiet.

Classrooms buzz with sound. There's the clatter of active play, the chatter of toddlers eating a snack, and the cry of an infant as she transitions to sleep. All this is set against a backdrop of adults' calm voices. At various times, children need space to make noise and space to be quiet, and the environment accommodates for that. The cozy reading area is far from the cacophony of the music and block-building areas. Teachers monitor classroom noise and neither chat constantly among themselves nor play music incessantly. This allows children to focus on important sounds, such as friends' voices, the teacher reading aloud, and the sounds of nature from outdoors. As shown in the photo to the right, one of our infant rooms has windows that look out onto the Patagonia café. Visitors touring the Patagonia headquarters often stop at these windows, because it's unique to see an infant and toddler play area in a place of business.

When [children] have enough space, safe space, they will do exactly the movements that they are ready for—because they have the opportunity. — *Magda Gerber*

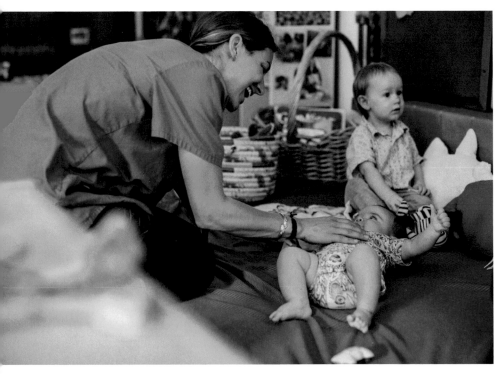

Background noise is a challenge for children developing language skills.

New research indicates that background noise can hinder how children learn. Experiments on speech perception done at the University of North Carolina revealed that toddlers found noise more distracting than adults did. Young children can hear almost too well in a noisy environment and miss parts of what is said; this can pose problems for language development. In contrast, in noisy environments, when adults can't hear every single word, they have the ability to substitute logical words and get the gist of a conversation.

Dr. Rochelle Newman of the University of Maryland offers tips to "turn down the volume" and ensure young children can focus and listen:

— Speak clearly, and make eye contact with children.

— When there is background noise, let children see your lips when talking.

— If they don't appear to understand, try again with simpler words.

— Behavior problems at school can be related to not being able to hear or understand the teacher.

— Don't leave TV, radio, or other speaking electronics on as background.

We have more caregivers and smaller class sizes.

One crucial structural element that allows for flexibility is a low number of students per caregiver or teacher. We have small class sizes and more teachers (one teacher to three infants or toddlers; one teacher to six two-year-olds; one teacher to eight three-year-olds+). Having one-on-one primary caregivers and small group sizes gives teachers the time they need to observe students, bond with them, and adapt programs and the environment as needed. This allows each child to blossom in a homelike environment.

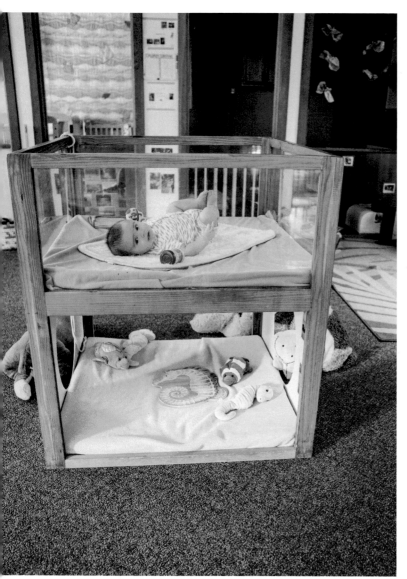

The baby tier gives immobile infants independence.

The baby tier is furniture built specifically for the center that keeps immobile babies (called "floor babies") safe when adults step away, and it allows floor babies uninterrupted solo play. We use baby tiers inside and out, and each has a bottom portion where babies can play. Babies who can push up on their hands and knees or roll over in succession are no longer placed in the baby tier.

Quiet nap rooms are for nursing and sleeping.

Infants sleep on their own schedules, so we have separate nap rooms adjacent to the classroom. From the main classroom area, teachers can see children in their cribs, so sleeping children are consistently observed. Each infant has a specific crib, and each toddler has his or her own sleeping mat. In the photo above (right), the baby has

mastered rolling from her back to tummy and has moved into her preferred sleeping position. A light blanket is available at her feet if necessary. The nap room is a peaceful place where nursing mothers can feed their babies or spend a quiet moment together.

In inclement weather, young children play outside on a patio.

The infant and toddler patio has a quiet-play area, climbing equipment, and pushcarts, plus spaces for group and solo play. Having a patio gives younger children options. When it's wet or windy, children can choose to play inside in the classroom or outside on the patio.

The patio connects to the older children's yard. For licensing requirements, a separation exists between the two, but the older children often stop by and chat with younger children through the barrier.

Purposeful chaos in the backyard.

Every classroom, even the infants', has a play area that allows for natural outdoor experiences. We have several gardens, which are always available for tending. Each day, the infant and toddler yard is set up with toys and activities to spark creative play. Children sweep leaves, gather pine cones, and explore dramatic play in the gazebo. Rolling down and climbing back up the steep hill is a rite of passage for toddlers.

Two- to three-year-olds need spaces blending pretend and physical play.

A climbing ladder and slide, a corner to be alone, a creative expression area, and a place for socializing—these spaces support the broad range of activities two- to three-year-olds enjoy and need. Pretend play becomes as important as physical play when children turn two, so their classroom has props for dress-up and playacting, as well as a structure for climbing. Two-year-olds are transitioning from mostly playing alone to interacting regularly with others, therefore teachers create spaces for both independent and small-group play.

A little bit of everything: the two- to three-year-olds' yard.

Infants, toddlers, and two- to three-year-olds play in the "Dolphin Yard" surrounded by activity centers as well as our vegetable, flower, and fruit gardens. A staple of the outdoor classroom, the messy kitchen is stocked with natural materials and household items. It's a model environment because it engages children in so many aspects of learning-filled play. We've watched children mix sand and dirt, add water, drop in five leaves, submerge their hands in the mucky concoction to mix it up, and then, with the help of a friend, carry the heavy bowl to the "oven." This is how the messy kitchen engages children in science, math, sensory exploration, fine and gross motor activities, and pretend play.

Areas for growing independence: the three- to four-year-olds' rooms.

Independence and self-reliance are themes of the three- to four-year-olds' classroom. Routines include sharing and circle time, which are developmentally appropriate, as are desks for writing. As seen to the right, there's an art area stocked with pens, markers, pencils, scissors, tape, and paper (of all types and sizes), as well as recycled materials to spark creative expression. Children help prepare for meals and also set up their mats at nap time; small sinks and toilets encourage autonomy around basic tasks. Cubbies contain clothing; children can change garments as they see fit. The shared courtyard between the three- and four-year-old classrooms houses the largest gardens. Children cultivate lettuces, eggplant, tomatoes, green beans, peas, squash, and pumpkins, which are eaten as snacks or taken home to share with family members.

We use rating scales to critique our classrooms.

To evaluate our classrooms, we use the Infant Toddler Environment Rating Scale (ITERS), the Early Childhood Environment Rating Scale (ECERS), and the School-Age Care Environment Rating Scale (SACERS). These scales assess and rate everything from the furniture size to the appropriate number of toys per child, to the number of observable teacher and child interactions. GPCDC is a high-scoring center, so students and teachers from local colleges and preschools visit to observe our practices.

Spaces to challenge four- and five-year-olds.

Four-year-olds are industrious, purposeful, and equipped with verbal abilities to articulate what they need for their elaborate plans. Their classroom is adaptable, shifting to fit their changing interests. Materials and activities reflect the needs of older children who enjoy writing in journals, solving intricate puzzles, exploring mixed-media creative projects, and reading books. In addition, children at this age decide when or if they want to take a nap. Every classroom has a bulletin board to keep parents informed on a range of topics, including curricula (based on areas of development), classroom activities, and general announcements. Family photos hang in each classroom (at eye level for children) to build a connection between home and school.

Unstructured play on the Trolley Yard.

The Trolley Yard is the heart of our preschool—it bustles with wild play and child-led projects. Within the Trolley Yard is a large dramatic-play gazebo, which offers space where dinners are served, veterinarians check on stuffed animals, and books are read to baby dolls. The Trolley Yard has tree stumps, boulders, and fallen logs to practice balance and agility. It is filled with swings, sand, a stage, tricycles, scooters, balance bikes, climbing equipment, musical instruments, and a water pump. A place for children to engage their imaginations and senses, as kids use the space, its entire contents becomes the stuff of creative play.

Elements of the outdoor classroom are many.

Every area of the outdoor classroom has careful planning and consideration behind it. Even elements as simple as the bikes contribute to children's play and development on many levels. Bikes are, of course, good for physical development. We buy tandem bikes so that children can use them together and incorporate them into pretend play. Each child brings a helmet from home, which is stored on the yard. Children care for their own helmets by retrieving them and putting them away, which builds a sense of responsibility.

We accommodate creative expression of all sorts.

The stage is a place of somatic exploration and social interaction—dedicated to music and creative physical expression. Here, children incorporate familiar parts of their world with imagination to create adventurous story lines that they act out together: "Let's pack the gear into the car so we can drive to Yosemite!" They act, dance, wiggle, shake, shimmy, or take giant leaps into the air.

Messy kitchen and the "ship" inspire imagination.

The Trolley Yard features a messy kitchen, and it's where children role-play activities involving food, cooking, and more. On the "ship," children have access to blocks, building materials, and loose parts. When teachers notice a consistent theme, they place items (e.g., maps, telescopes, fabric) along with the existing objects to encourage play. While the "ship" is always industrious, the kitchen is a quieter retreat.

The secret area: solo play is imperative.

Children crave places where they can be in their own world—a world that's free from the eyes of adults. Of course, teachers supervise each play area at all times, but they also create the illusion of a private, magical world so that children can feel independent and have some privacy. In the secret area, there is a science center, a climbing wall and climbing tree, plus a fairy garden full of natural materials and magical plants. Quiet play areas offer nooks to create, among other things, dinosaur worlds and other elaborate fantasy adventures. The science area offers a place of observation, and the climbing wall under the trees gives children a private place to challenge themselves. Solo play is the focus; teachers intervene only if necessary.

A little calm amid an active play yard.

This cozy, quiet space adjacent to the secret area allows children some downtime from the action of the yard. Teachers are always nearby and available to read to children. A soft space with pillows, rugs, furniture, books, and friends is nestled under trees to create a soothing reading area. Anything we can do inside, we can also do outside.

Kids' Club: five- to eight-year-olds in charge.

School-age children are picked up after school. GPCDC teachers drive the vans that transport children from various elementary campuses to Kids' Club. Here the children have a snack, and then they are free to play indoors or out. The environment emphasizes self-reliance and accountability, and it features more complex activities and materials. Teachers focus on children's responsibility and their place within the community.

An environment that's just right for older kids.

Similar to the play yards for younger children, Kids' Club features gardens, fruit trees, building materials, sand, and climbing equipment. However, the climbing structures are taller and require more strength and skill, plus the children use very large building materials to create giant forts—the play is more sophisticated and riskier.

Children need the freedom and time to play. Play is not a luxury. Play is a necessity.

— *Kay Redfield Jamison*

What can rich sensory experiences teach children?

Chapter Seven: Learning through Our Senses

A rich sensory life not only creates joy and meaning, but it's how kids learn to reason, think, and feel. We hear, taste, see, feel, and smell the world—all of human experience is sensory. We use internal representations of senses by picturing things or retelling conversations in our mind. Lesser-known but crucial sensory systems also develop in early childhood: the vestibular system, which detects movement and gravitational pull; and proprioception, which gathers information about the body in space.

"Everything [children] see, hear, feel, touch, or even smell impacts their brain and thus influences the way they view and interact with their world—including their family, neighbors, strangers, friends, classmates, and even themselves." —*Daniel J. Siegel*

We use the natural world to explore all of the senses.

The natural world is the best source of sensory delight. It's filled with bird calls, sunlight, prickly grass, and ripe strawberries. As Richard Louv writes, "Any natural place contains an infinite reservoir of information and, therefore, the potential for inexhaustible new discoveries." Our yards are especially rich in fragrant plants: rosemary, mint, sunflowers, and geraniums.

Children live through their senses ... Since the natural environment is the principal source of sensory stimulation, freedom to explore or play with the outdoor environment through senses in their own space and time is essential for healthy development of an interior life. — *Robin Moore*

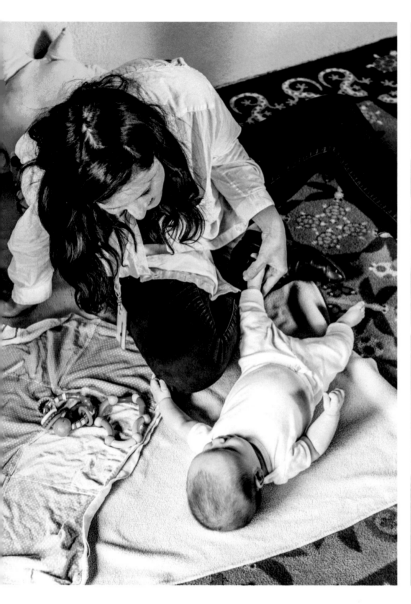

The sense of touch is key to overall development.

Psychologist Nancy Dess underscores the importance of human touch: "Without touch, infant primates die; adult primates with touch deficits become more aggressive." Young children fail to thrive without human touch, and they want to touch everything around them. Children, still developing their tactile systems, strengthen their brain with each new experience.

Playing with sand is a powerful sensory experience.

Dry sand runs through fingers smoothly and quickly. Wet sand can be molded and coats everything. It also dries quickly and forms "sand rocks," crumbling to the touch. Sand can be made into waterways, volcanoes, food, potions, and pools. It's so flexible that children transmute sand again and again, transforming themselves in the process. Children internalize the language they hear, so teachers narrate actions to build language concepts about sensory experiences. **Teachers say:** "As sand runs through your hand, it feels grainy and dry," or "Your feet are covered in sand. Does that make them feel warmer or colder?"

The sense of smell is ancient and linked to other senses.

Smell is the most primal human sense and is strongly connected to memory and emotion. The brain evolved from a pair of olfactory glands, so smell is an ancient sense linking us to the rest of the animal kingdom. The nose is responsible for much of our sense of taste, picking up 10,000 more flavors than the tongue. Acclimating children to a wide range of smells can also create adventurous eaters.

Smell is a potent wizard that transports you across thousands of miles and all the years you have lived. — *Helen Keller*

Taste is infants' gateway to the world.

The mouth is one of the first organs to appear in human embryos and continues to be primary in babies, who put items in their mouths to gather information. Taste continues to be a strong and emotional sense for young children. The language of tastes and textures is vast—sour, sweet, lively, tart, savory, smooth, crunchy, warm, and cold. Sometimes we talk about listening to ourselves chew: "Crunchy foods are loud!" Our fruit and vegetable snacks and child-accessible gardens help kids develop a taste for healthy and strong-flavored foods.

above: Fall Catalog 1990 — Uli Wiesmeier

Eyesight matures during the first two years of life.

Humans are not born with a fully developed sense of sight. Newborns can't control focus, eye movement, or use their eyes in tandem. Their visual development goes through radical growth in the first two years of life; therefore, young children especially relish interesting visual experiences. They will squat down to see underneath something to discover hidden objects. They will marvel at looking through binoculars, because it allows them to see details of objects faraway. Delighted and attached to visual imagery, children sometimes express intense reactions when they can't have a desired color or texture.

Changing children's perspective reveals alternate points of view.

To view the world from other vantage points allows children to see life differently than they normally do, sparking imagination and encouraging abstract reasoning. We play a game called *Do I Fit?* to challenge children's perceptions of size and space. Two-year-olds choose an item in the room and see if they fit in it. It's interesting to watch young children as they recognize what's too big, too small, or too ridiculous for their bodies. Teachers offer nonjudgmental narration. **Teachers say:** "Do you fit in the wooden oven when you're standing? How about if you crouch? I see you crawling through a tiny opening to get inside that long, narrow box. Do you fit?"

Messy sensory experiences inspire creativity and imagination.

Full sensory experiences are often messy. The value of sensory play outweighs any individual teacher's tolerance for mess. We intentionally offer messy activities, ensuring kids get the sensory input they crave. Nontoxic paint is rich in color for the eyes and texture for the sense of touch. Teachers set up the materials so that children can get it between fingers and toes, even in mouths. All surfaces can be canvases, including the body.

Messy play is preparation for the unexpected.

— Jennifer Ridgeway

Playing with water and ice teaches children about their properties.

Everyone remembers the joy of playing with water as a kid. Running fingers through chilly waves. Floating pieces of driftwood, watching the ripples dance alongside. The plopping sounds of heavy rocks dropped in a pond. Moving hands through water provides resistance, contributing to proprioceptive development. The physical repetition of water play can be soothing to children. Teachers offer unstructured, open-ended water play indoors and out. Children help make ice and watch the water transform from liquid to solid. They enjoy embedding treasures in ice blocks and playing out scenarios to rescue the treasures from the ice. We discuss melting and use vocabulary like *cold*, *temperature*, and *freeze*. **Teachers say:** "You're exploring the ice with your fingers. What does it feel like? Brrr, it's cold!"

Rain is joyful and engages all the senses.

Our teachers follow this maxim: There is no inclement weather, only inappropriate clothing. Our children don their boots and raincoats and play in the rain. Despite having the proper gear, children often get soaked, but they change into dry clothes, which we always have on hand. Playing in the rain is a rite of passage—even in Southern California, where it rarely rains. When it does, children are ecstatic and rush outside to feel the droplets on their faces and tongues, to jump in puddles, and to smell the renewed air.

Children delight in playing with water, soap, and bubbles.

Not all sensory play must be mucky. Soap and water are part of children's daily routine, but when provided on a larger scale, children delight in popping bubbles and creating foam. Kids slip easily into dramatic play, washing the dolls and other toys to emulate their bathing rituals. Blowing bubbles requires children to take deep breaths, so it can also help kids relax. Wielding bubble wands of various sizes strengthens kids' fine motor skills. Bubbles, pearlescent orbs, floating delicately until by invisible forces they pop, evoke wonder and laughter in all ages.

Children sculpt with soft paper rolls and transform their environment.

Soft paper offers a different experience from a flat sheet of paper. Paper rolls can be sculpted, rolled, and draped around the body. When thrown, they float, landing silently. Long rolls allow children to connect various areas of a room and transform space on a vast scale. Large sensory environments spark children's imaginations in a big way.

Children use the proprioception system to know where they are in the world.

With eyes closed, ears plugged, and without touching anything, we can tell where our body is and what shape it's in; this is proprioception. It is the sense of the body moving in space, and it entails positioning, movement, and joint pressure. Biting and chewing also use proprioception. When children jump and play, they gather infor-

mation about lengthening and contracting muscles. They lift things to learn how much strength is needed and practice how hard to push a pencil tip or pick up a paper cup without crushing the object. Learning to position the body is crucial to navigating the physical world successfully.

The vestibular system is essential and allows us to feel grounded.

The vestibular sense uses the inner ear to detect movement and gravitational pull. It's the first sensory system to develop fully, and, as it coordinates information from other senses, it influences almost everything we do. If you've had a case of vertigo, which is a disruption of the vestibular system, then you know it's almost impossible to function without it. Getting lots of sensory stimulation to the vestibular system is crucial. Flipping upside-down challenges the vestibular system, and we also encourage games and provide equipment that exercise the vestibular system, including rolling, spinning, balance beam, hammock, slides, ball play, and freeze games. The children control the speed at which they spin or rock.

All our knowledge begins with the senses. —*Immanuel Kant*

Dancing helps children control their bodies.

Dancers who refine the art of moving the body in space for years have very well-developed proprioceptive systems. We dance with children daily. We have many dance parties and create improvisational games so that children can play with movement, enjoying and developing control of the body as it's moving through space.

The inexpressible depth of music, so easy to understand and yet so inexplicable, is due to the fact that it reproduces all the emotions of our innermost being. — *Oliver Sacks*

Children enjoy playing with sound and music—and it does them good.

Research now shows that quality music programs teach children more than music. They improve reading, language, and math skills. Children delight in music and unexpected sounds. They love to imitate what they hear or imagine: the whirring of a motor, the drone of a siren, or the roar of a lion. Much of play is ebullient and loud, while another type of play requires quiet focus. Teachers carefully consider how to deal with both.

Music is the universal language of mankind. — *Henry Wadsworth Longfellow*

— Our music teacher, Annie, shares how —
children respond to music

A Feast for the Senses

Music has all the essentials of education. It stimulates emotions, coordination, and movement and can build self-esteem and social skills. A 2012 study of one-year-old infants found that interactive music classes led to better communication. Babies who learned to play percussion instruments and sang songs with their parents showed a greater sensitivity to musical structures and tones. Very young children exposed to music education had better early communication skills—like waving good-bye or pointing to an object they wanted. In our music classes, we practice finding the correct pitch, timing, rhythmic patterning, rhyming, and music vocabulary. Children enjoy playing different instruments, singing children's songs, and creating songs themselves. Together we explore many styles of music from different cultures.

Each year, I bring in two old Italian accordions and show how they are held and played. The accordion, with its keys and buttons, is not a percussion instrument like the piano—it's a wind instrument like the harmonica. We lay the huge, heavy accordions on the ground and discuss the parts and how each works. Children take turns extending an accordion and pressing the buttons and keys. I remember bringing the accordions to the four-year-olds' room, and a child shouted out, "Those are the bellows!" He was pointing at the accordion's folding air chambers. I asked how he knew so much, and he said, "From you, teacher Annie, when I was a Sea Star." He had remembered a music lesson from when he was three years old. Something comes through to children when they interact with music. I think children grow up much more confident when they have quality music education.

What is creativity?

Chapter Eight: Inspiring Creativity

Creativity is an essential part of lifelong learning, and we're all born with the potential for imaginative innovation. Unfortunately, most schools do not provide the time, the space, or the encouragement children need to express their vibrant perceptions. In addition, well-meaning adults inhibit a child's natural curiosity when they offer "drawing advice" or give a child a coloring book. We are inspired by and indebted to Viktor Lowenfeld and W. L. Brittain, pioneers in art education. Since the 1940s, their definitive book *Creative and Mental Growth* has been essential in university and college credentialing programs for art teachers. Unfortunately, the textbook is less known outside of academic circles. For our part, we've given copies of it to teachers and new parents for decades, and now we've condensed the main themes into art "dos and don'ts." We emphasize the value of asking open-ended questions such as "Tell me about this," rather than the almost reflexive and quite detrimental "What are you drawing?"; "Is that a boat?"; or "Are those waves?" Open-ended questions and comments focus on the child's goal of joyfully transforming simple materials, rather than the adult's interest in product production. How do adults inspire creativity in children? This chapter offers suggestions. Whether a child is drawing in the sand with a stick or with a crayon on the wall, adults will know what to say.

"To teach toward creativity is to teach toward the future of society." *— Lowenfeld and Brittain*

Creativity is developed through divergent thinking.

Convergent thinking asks, "What color is this?" Divergent thinking asks, "What color would you like it to be?" The crux of creativity is the ability to answer one question in many ways. Creativity is less concerned with the "right" way to produce a product than the unique perception, feelings, and thoughts that lead to the inspiration. Creativity means we trust ourselves to ask, "What else can I try? What else might this mean to me?" Teachers cultivate divergent thinking through a variety of questions that inspire the imagination and incite self-reflection. Adults who nurture a spirit of experimentation have mastered divergent classroom discussions.

Divergent questions are useful when children are stuck.

A child stares at a palette of paints and says, "I don't know what color to pick." Teachers can help by asking open-ended questions. **Teachers say:** "I wonder what you can do when you feel stuck? I wonder what color you keep looking at? Are there colors you see around you that might help you choose?" The questions don't have a correct answer; they broaden the child's frame of reference, inviting him to go deeper into his experience. Nearby children chime in, "When I get stuck, I think about my blanket and pick red." This sparks discussion, and soon a group of children and the teacher are talking about the ways they pick colors. Discussions and answers from multiple perspectives encourage innovation.

Divergent

Convergent

Coloring books affect
a child's creative expression

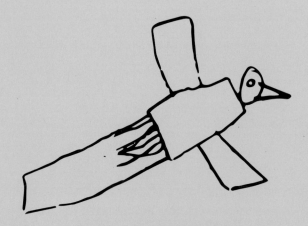

Fig. 1 Before being exposed to coloring books, a child drew this picture of a bird.

Fig. 2 The child was then asked to copy and color a workbook illustration of birds.

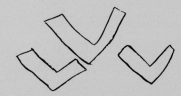

Fig. 3 After coloring the birds in the workbook, the same child draws more birds, but now he attempts to copy the workbook illustration, not the birds of his imagination.

Children who have suffered adult interferences are the ones who will constantly ask questions on how to use the materials, and are easily influenced by the work of others. They will lack self-confidence. They are the ones most easily damaged by coloring books. *— Lowenfeld and Brittain*

According to experimental studies by Russell and Waugaman, 63 percent of the children exposed to workbooks and coloring books lost their initial ability to draw birds. The children realize that they could never draw a bird as expertly, so believing they can't compete, they quite logically decide, *I can't draw*.

Many adults find coloring books a restful meditation. Parents, when confronted with the studies, say, "But my children love coloring books!" They might, but kids don't always know what is good for them—we don't allow them to eat candy all day. And we protect children's creativity by encouraging confidence in their abilities to struggle through creating original forms and ideas.

*Drawings courtesy of Dr. Irene Russell, *Research Bulletin*, The Eastern Arts Association, Vol. 3, No. 1, 1952 in *Creative and Mental Growth*, Eighth Edition, by Vicktor Lowenfeld and W. Lambert Brittain

Art is not the same for children as it is for adults.

Art for a preschool-age child is an action experiment, not a product. Adults enjoy creating products. Adults comment about products. Young children are confused by adults' unattainable product standards.

Children move through visible art stages that coincide with their cognitive development. Knowing how to recognize each stage provides adults with a tangible view into each child's progress toward maturation.

No one is born creative, but everyone is capable of developing their own creativity.

Creativity, like love, can flourish or be crushed. Just as a variety of foods builds our bodies, creative intelligence grows through exposure to a variety of enriching experiences. Toddlers spend many of their waking hours experimenting with cause and effect. Scribbling is the result of a struggle to first perceive, then gain enough hand-eye coordination to control the production of their lines called scribbling.

Offer creative experiences, not adult-directed, product-focused projects.

The cut-paper snowman, handprints transformed into turkeys, and other such cookie-cutter art projects discourage young children who can't complete them on their own. Instead, teachers can give children paper of different sizes—from the length of a wall to tiny notes. Present paper on various surfaces, such as the floor, the table, or taped to a wall. Three-dimensional surfaces, like cardboard boxes, are also enticing when offered with wide, dark markers.

We cannot positively affect children's behavior by giving them patterns or procedures to follow in order to achieve "better-looking" product. The change in the product itself should come about through the changes in a child's thinking, feeling, and perceiving.

— *Lowenfeld and Brittain*

Scribbling stage: the beginnings of self-control.

Although the word connotes a lack of care, scribbling is a key step in the development of the human brain. Scribbling goes through several stages that can look visually similar but have very different meaning to the scribbling child. Understanding what scribblers experience and express is important to knowing what to say and what materials to offer.

A child who appears fearful of drawing might have been punished for breaking crayons, or wasting paper.

— *Lowenfeld and Brittain*

It's easy to break a child's scribbling stage.

Scribblers don't set out to draw anything. Asking, "What are you drawing? What is it?" implies that children should be drawing something, which confuses or discourages. Instead, caregivers should narrate the child's actions.

Caregivers say: "I see you moving your hand in a circle." or "You're lifting your hand up and down, which makes tiny dots on the page."

If a child then creates what you consider beautiful art, but wants to scribble all over it, let her. Stopping any creative act casts doubt and can contribute to insecurity. Early creation is an expression of empowerment, enjoyment, and cognitive development.

Scribbling is about line; color choice is incidental.

Scribbling children are studying line. Therefore, scribbling is best supported with simple materials, like black crayon on white paper, or chalk on blackboard.

Scribblers will enjoy colors if offered. But color sensory play is better supported with activities like mixing colored water or messy painting. Similarly, very goopy, oily, or slippery art supplies, while good for sensory play, are frustrating to scribblers. The clearer the line, the more children internalize the lessons that scribbling offers.

Disordered scribbling: a laboratory of the senses.

Young children experiment with materials for pleasure. By looking, feeling, smelling—even tasting—they discover what materials do. Putting crayon to paper requires knowledge of grasp, pressure, speed, and movement. Children learn to connect their bodies and senses with tools by working and struggling with them. Early scribblers don't yet realize that they are the ones who are making marks appear on the page. The best way to talk to early scribblers is to narrate what the child is doing.

Caregivers say: "You're moving your hand so fast back and forth. You're holding a marker. How does it feel in your hand? Is it smooth or rough?"

At this phase, adults should offer the same materials for longer periods. Switching materials too quickly can frustrate early scribblers, who are just learning to master hand-eye coordination.

On his own, the young child will gain visual and physical control of his scribblings by two years of age.

— *Lowenfeld and Brittain*

Controlled scribbling: understanding they're making a mark.

Imagine this: After about six months of scribbling, you look down and realize you are responsible for the marks on the page. Then consider how your feelings of power would turn to dismay if your first experience of artistic self-accomplishment was met with suggestions for improvement. Success at producing their "mark" bolsters two-year-olds' growing sense of independence. Controlled scribbling is a visible sign of remarkable changes; the child's brain is now able to turn thoughts into action.

Named scribbling: symbolic thinking begins.

When children name their drawings, "This is my doggy," they've reached the final scribbling phase. Named scribbling coincides with kids' growing abilities to play with objects symbolically. "Let's pretend this box is a car" is the same thing as calling a line "Mommy." Although these children now label drawings, they aren't trying to draw what they see. Named scribbling is an imaginative game, which is why children will call the same drawing many things: "It's a pumpkin," then, "It's a sea monster, it's a dragon!"

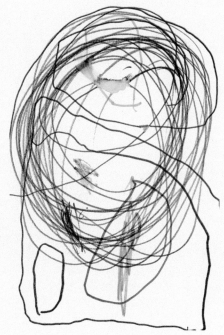

I Made a Happy Face

Preschematic: intentionally drawing shapes and naming them.

In the preschematic stage, preschoolers begin to draw circles and squares in addition to more defined images than scribblers. They also begin to name them: "Look, it's the sun. Now it's a rocket." In this stage, children don't have a strong logical grasp of space, so objects float on the page, and kids rotate their paper while working. Preschematic children have a growing sense of identity and connection, which gets expressed through their own symbols.

Characteristics of the preschematic stage:

Art is a communication with self

Shapes are geometric

Placement and size of objects are subjective—they float about

Objects are not related to each other by size

Paper is rotated while drawing

Head and feet grow from scribbles; gradually arms and other body parts emerge from head

If a child is in the scribbling or preschematic stage, he or she is not ready to read.

— Lowenfeld and Brittain

Preschematic: fantasy in search of order.

Preschematic children see themselves as the center of everything, including their drawings. They draw objects as they relate to them, with no concern for how objects relate spatially to one another. Before drawing, to help inspire their imaginations, discuss topics that emphasize children's relationships: their relationships to themselves, to loved ones, and to their senses. Lowenfeld and Brittain report that children drew pictures on the following topics after these types of discussions.

Lowenfeld and Brittain cite these examples of children's artwork after discussions:

Me and my mother.

Me and my family.

Me and my house.

I am brushing my teeth.

I am drinking my milk.

I am blowing my nose.

I hurt my knee.

I am picking flowers.

I am eating breakfast.

My Pregnant Mommy

Schematic stage: the dawning of logic.

The schematic stage is important because the ability to create fixed symbols demonstrates that children have entered a new period of logical thinking. It doesn't occur overnight, but logical thinking increases as the child's brain develops.

Art is a way of learning, as relationships are figured out during the act of drawing. A challenging activity, it must be meaningful for the youngster. *— Lowenfeld and Brittain*

Schematic: the stage of fixed symbols.

The schematic stage evolves slowly as children begin to develop certain set forms, almost like prefabricated parts that act as their personal symbols for certain objects. For example, the child always draws people using a circle for the head, an oval-shaped body, four lines for the arms and legs, and two dots and a half circle for the face. The schematic child draws the same figure, regardless of the shape, size, or age of the person they're representing. Each child's set of schemas is unique and is influenced by that child's feelings and experiences.

Characteristics of the schematic stage:

A baseline that objects rest on

Toward the end of preschematic stage, clothing, hair, and body parts have begun to develop

Bold, direct, and flat representations

An active awareness of the child's environment

Little or no overlapping

Body made of geometric shapes

Arms and legs develop volume and correct placement

Proportions are exaggerated and depend on emotional value

Schematic children organize space on a baseline.

As Lowenfeld and Brittain put it, "The great discovery of the five- to nine-year-old, is that there is an order in space." Children at this stage start drawing baselines: A line or lines across the bottom of the page represents the ground and is often accompanied by a corresponding line above for the sky. Scenes take place in a flat plane between the two. Size is still relative and reflects the emotional life of the child, rather than the physical reality—the child draws herself taller than the house, the tree, and her older sister because her own experience looms large. Children of the same age will not always be at the same stage. The child on the left is evolving into preschematic. In contrast, the child on the right draws a picture with sky and ground symbols and is therefore beginning the schematic stage.

Camping with Poppa

Schematic children are ready to learn to read.

Knowing that a drawing of a tree can be used to represent all trees is the same as understanding that c-a-t always refers to cat and the letter a indicates a short a sound. Using a baseline also means that children can begin to differentiate between letters like b and d—an essential skill for literacy. Schematic drawing is a by-product of cognitive development, but it doesn't create cognitive development.

Though preschematic children might successfully imitate schematic drawing, they won't develop the necessary thinking until their brain is ready. Premature efforts to teach symbols often causes "acting out" as a result of boredom and fearful resistance to symbols that can affect reading and math development.

Personal schemas have codified color and design.

Children at the schematic stage use shapes *and* colors symbolically. They paint the sky blue even if it's a cloudy day; they color the grass green when the lawn is brown. Children in this stage resist alternative color suggestions and may become frustrated when colors accidentally blend. Adults need not fear a child's rigid color choice; this actually indicates a growing capacity to think logically and symbolically.

Although design elements may appear in schematic work, they are only there to serve the children's schema. Children have little interest in learning technique. Art at this stage is for the purpose of developing symbols and stories to better understand their own experiences.

Schematic

Repetitive drawing is an opportunity go deeper into subject matter.

When kids get comfortable drawing a particular image—a flower or a rocket—they might start drawing it over and over. This sometimes worries adults, who then ask, "Why don't you draw something besides a rocket?" The child who draws the same object again and again is unsure about his ability, then feels pressured and insecure. Instead, teachers can ask questions about the image.

Teachers say: "Where is that rocket going? I wonder what it will find when it gets there? This rocket is big, and this one is small—what's the difference between them? I wonder how this rocket works? Who is riding inside?"

Increase creative confidence with tailor-made art activities.

For a child who repeatedly draws or paints the same thing, such as a rocket ship, the teacher can set up a rocket-ship play area. The child might enjoy making the rocket out of recycled materials, clay, wood or a collage of materials. These kinds of experiences foster deep relationships between the child and his drawing. Often the child decides to include the astronaut or control panel, and the image becomes quite detailed. As the artwork gets more complex, the child gains confidence in his abilities and starts depicting different subjects.

Get children engaged before any creative process.

Lowenfeld and Brittain suggest discussing feelings and the topic in general before children begin to draw or paint. The goal is to foster a creative atmosphere that is open and flexible to any suggestions from the child. If children cannot think of anything to draw, teachers can subtly suggest subject matter by discussing children's lives with a spirit of discovery.

Teachers say: "When do you play? Didn't I just see you playing? Who was there? Where? Could you use the whole field to play? Did you just stand there, or were you running after something? Do you stand tall and straight when you run? Oh, you would fall over running like that? Show me how you run fast. If you lean over too far, what happens? Would you fall on your knee? Would it hurt? Would it bleed?"

When children are "stuck," teachers can inspire the creative process.

Connect to their world.

Children are often inspired to talk about and create art about their experiences. Teachers can ask questions that spark discussions about time spent with others, action, and location. Lowenfeld and Brittain report that children created art on the following topics after discussions that connected them to their world.

Lowenfeld and Brittain cite these examples of children's artwork after discussions:

We went to the zoo.

Playing with my friends on the school grounds.

Jumping over a rope held by Bob and John.

I am climbing a tree.

Pulling myself high on the playground rings.

We are sledding down a hill.

We are planting a garden.

We are cooking dinner.

Playing ball with my friends.

Going camping with my mother and dad.

Grocery shopping with my dad.

We are climbing a mountain.

Small moments can inspire creative expression.

As inspiration for creative personal expression, teachers should look for moments during play to later recall with children.

Teachers say: "What did you do? Where were you? Was it difficult? Was it fun?"

Lowenfeld and Brittain cite these examples of children's artwork after discussions:

Holding onto the rope while swinging.

Playing checkers with my friend.

Talking with my mother.

Eating breakfast across the table from my brother.

Holding an umbrella in one hand and my books in the other.

Watching the parade go by.

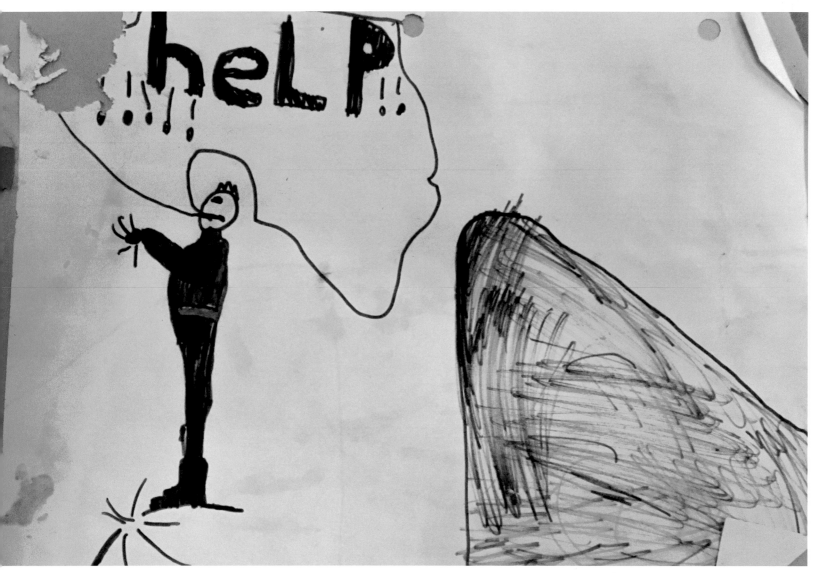

Drawing by an eight-year-old of "The Broken Ski."

Remembering events helps children consider space and time.

Discussing memorable events from kid's lives encourages them to place their work in space and time. **Teachers say:** "When did this happen? Where did this happen?"

Lowenfeld and Brittain cite these examples of children's artwork after discussions:

We eat together at school.

Our trip to the police department.

When we went to visit the farm.

We helped bake bread.

Challenge children to represent the world in an X-ray format.

Children of this age enjoy exploring layers of space. When you ask them about their home or buildings they know, they often then begin representing the world in an X-ray format. They will likely depict both indoor and outdoor cross sections.

Lowenfeld and Brittain cite these examples of children's artwork after discussions:

My parents and I stay in a hotel.

We visit different floors of Mom's office.

My friends and I explore an old cow barn.

My stay at the hospital.

My father and I visit the hardware store.

How I broke my leg.

Trying to build a tree fort.

left: An example of X-ray format: a six-year-old draws an outline of a house and its interior.

Encourage flexibility in schematic children.

Although schematic children are fairly rigid about color selection, conversations that evoke color subtly encourage them to broaden their palettes. Before children draw, teachers can ask questions about color and texture. **Teachers say:** "Did anyone walking in the leaves find a red, yellow, or orange leaf?" or "Let's go outside and count the clouds. What do you see?"

Lowenfeld and Brittain cite these examples of children's artwork after discussions:

We find bright colors in the fall.

We like to play in the rain.

The workmen are painting our house.

The new grass is beginning to grow after the rains.

We got our new shoes covered with mud.

The new puppies were all different from each other.

The new garden flowers surprised us with their colors.

I went shopping for new clothes.

Never criticize children's artwork.

Children's inner emotions are of deep concern to them. Adults must be careful not to criticize or comment on any artwork; special care should be given to emotional subjects.

Lowenfeld and Brittain cite these examples of children's artwork after discussions:

The time I was most afraid.

If I could do anything I wanted to do for one day.

Once I had a terrible dream.

I make believe I am an animal.

If I were a teacher.

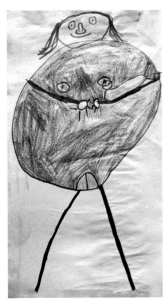

Mama has a new baby.

Never stop a child who is working to tell him the correct method.

Experimenting with various materials can foster flexibility. Adults must put aside their ideas on how the materials should be used and encourage children to discover their approach. Don't offer examples of finished projects.

To develop a positive image of one's self, to encourage confidence in one's own means of expression, to provide opportunity for constructive divergent thinking should be the basic aims for any art program.

Lowenfeld and Brittain suggest the following lesson plan ideas:

Painting in light and dark colors.

Making a collage.

Making tall things with holes out of clay.

Making things from boxes and colored paper.

Using crayons in different ways.

Creating a rough and smooth picture.

It is essential that a child be given constant encouragement to explore and investigate new ways and methods.

— *Lowenfeld and Brittain*

Creative self-doubt starts in childhood.

Children who have been exposed to coloring books, misguided questions about their creative work, follow-the-directions art projects, and aesthetic praise too often may have already become creatively insecure. They will say, "Draw for me," or "I can't draw." To counteract early insecurity, offer kids a range of materials until they find one that doesn't stress them—it could be woodworking, printing, collage, or sculpting with clay. Notice which subjects interest the child, and encourage these by asking divergent questions. Soon the child will develop creative confidence that will eventually translate into building, drawing, dancing, music, painting, storytelling, and any other endeavors that require creativity.

A child's own efforts must be accepted and bolstered no matter how meager the product appears.

— *Lowenfeld and Brittain*

Art appreciation with kids is about making connections to life.

Open-ended questions build a dynamic personal relationship between children and art, be it their own or others'. **Teachers say:** "What does this remind you of? I wonder what's happening here? How does this make you feel? I wonder what's happening between those two dogs?"

Steer away from questions that analyze: "Why did you draw yourself much bigger than the house?" With practice, the emotional and imaginative sensitivity required to answer open-ended questions strengthens. Children's perceptions, curiosity, and flexibility about ideas grow as a result of their struggle toward creative confidence.

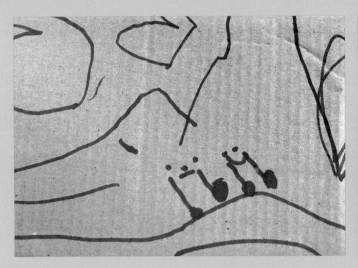

— Auntie Story —

Draw a Heart for Me!

I frequently babysit my three-year-old niece. Recently, she asked me to draw a heart for her. I countered, "Teach me how?" Several tantrums later she implored, "My hearts don't look like teacher's hearts." She was upset, and I was conflicted. I thought, *How big a deal could drawing a heart for her be?* And yet, I didn't want her to think that she couldn't draw her ideas. In desperation, I handed her a new box of wide-tipped, colored markers.

Excitement over the markers was a great relief to us. I asked questions about the colors, so no hearts were needed. But after comparing the colors, again she whined, "Draw a heart for me."

Instead I mused, "Would that cardboard box enjoy some colors?" She liked the idea, so I placed her three favorite markers in the big box and began tidying up, feigning disinterest.

I soon heard her narrating her drawings: "Here's his sock. Yes, it's so wet outside. Such cold feet." To my chagrin, she stopped drawing when I made an enthusiastic comment about her first-ever stick figure. I switched topics: "Would you like to see a trick with scissors and folded paper?" Making snowflakes consumed the afternoon.

The next day, I was astonished when she drew a baseline along her paper and, with great determination, narrated that there were " ... fairies and flowers by mountains ... ," which so recently had been unacceptable hearts. With her new snowflake skills, the fairies had skirts. What an unexpected development; what a leap from yesterday's tears.

Will she again get self-consciously stuck and demand adults draw for her? If so, it will now be easier to put art teacher theory into practice. I'm relieved I resisted showing off my heart-drawing skill, as now her misshapen hearts hang on my wall relabeled as "Mountains, with Fairies and Flowers."

Gross motor development happens naturally when an infant has plenty of space to move in a safe, age-appropriate, and challenging environment.

— *Stephanie Petrie*

Why should babies sit, crawl, stand, and walk at their own pace, in their own time?

Chapter Nine: Strengthening Bodies

Giving infants time, space, and skillful support to develop physically is crucial. As babies learn to move, they discover that they can affect themselves, objects, and other people. Each new skill—rolling over, sitting up, or crawling—lays the foundation for all areas of life: physically, mentally, and even socially. Respecting developmental stages is critical, so we never force infants to sit up or walk before they are ready to do so on their own, and we don't use walkers, jumpers, "activity" seats, or high chairs. Our teachers carefully track important physical milestones, because solid development of the body is the sound groundwork for life.

Floor time allows infants to gain control of their bodies.

During floor time, babies are placed on their backs and have uninterrupted time to move how they like. Infants reach, roll, and push up, all the while building confidence and autonomy. One of the first things infants learn to do is put their fingers and toes into their mouths. Caregivers arrange interesting selections of objects and toys on the floor, knowing that infants, eager explorers, will initiate movement in the direction of them. When they can roll to get what they desire, they have a greater sense of power and will. Magda Gerber

had the right idea: "Instead of trying to teach babies new skills, we appreciate and admire what babies are actually doing." In the photos to the right, a five-month-old works hard to maneuver from his back to his stomach. He reaches across his body, then kicks his opposing leg over and lets gravity do the rest. While infants move, caregivers provide encouragement. **Caregivers say:** "I see that you are becoming frustrated trying to roll over. You almost have it—just get that leg over and you'll be on your tummy. I'm right here for you."

Trust your baby's competence: She wants to do things for herself, and she *can* do things for herself. — *Stephanie Petrie*

Trust babies to learn to push up and pivot to sit in their own time.

Babies begin to roll onto their stomachs on their own, around the same time their arm, neck, and back muscles are strong enough to push up. This action begins the lifelong action of extending the spine upward, which will be needed for crawling and eventually standing. A few months later, these children use problem-solving skills and developing muscles to pivot into a sitting position. From all fours, infants rock back so that their legs are underneath them with their hands still on the floor. Once ready, they will pick up their hands and figure out where to place their legs for greater stability.

Crawling and pulling to stand are crucial steps not to be bypassed.

As babies crawl, their world changes. They can go where they want, and their social life expands as they approach others more often. Crawling requires a lot of neurological work. Crossing the body's midline, coordinating arms and legs, and contralateral movement are the basics of walking and develop connections between the two sides of the brain. When children pull to stand up, they coordinate their arms, legs, feet, and back. Once up, they view their surroundings from a new vantage point and can see others eye to eye.

Infants need a safe place to move and explore.

Our infant rooms allow newly crawling babies to explore everywhere. These environments are safe and accessible and don't inhibit infants' need to investigate. The rooms are full of heavy furniture that won't tip when babies use it to pull themselves up. In the photos above, an infant sees an intriguing toy on the table and pulls himself up to investigate. Infants can become frustrated or frightened when they are learning to move from a standing position to sitting and vice versa. Caregivers support them by positioning themselves closer and coaching them through the process. If a child needs more help, the caregiver stands next to him or her and allows the child to brace against the caregiver's body.

Learning to walk takes patience and time.

Walking, and ultimately running, takes practice and patience as children learn to balance in many positions and coordinate their movements. When children first walk, their gait is unsteady and arms are held wide for added balance. As skills are refined, children draw their arms in, move more intentionally, and seldom fall. On two feet, children feel triumphant, moving the way they've seen others do. For the first time, their hands are free while they move. On-site child care has many benefits, including being able to see baby's first steps. If possible, caregivers contact parents so they can be there for their children's major milestones.

All children accomplish milestones in their own way, in their own time.

— *Anita Garaway-Furtaw*

Pushing requires coordination and teaches kids about the physical world.

Children love to push because it allows them to physically control more than their own body. Pushing incorporates the coordinated use of arms and legs. For these children, successfully maneuvering means looking ahead for obstacles and steering accordingly.

By pushing items of different weights, children gather information about the world around them. They learn to maneuver around objects and other people.

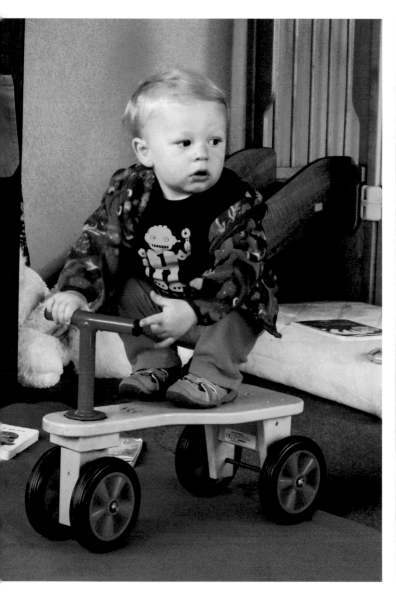

Balance combines physical control, vision, and body awareness.

Balance, the foundation of movement, is comprised of three elements: physical control, vision, and the awareness of the body in space (proprioception). The three systems develop slowly and in tandem. Children first learn to balance their head, then their trunk, and finally to incorporate their feet and legs. As they grow, kids rely more and more on their sense of balance, attempting increasingly daring feats; their success determined by the abilities they built as babies.

We help children learn to balance risk and safety.

Our environment and program encourage risk taking. The materials offer a range of challenges, so that children can incrementally increase risk. We offer classes like gymnastics, which promotes balance, flexibility, and controlled risk. Our older children take to the nearby bike path with skateboards, scooters, and roller skates. Teachers talk with children about their strategies for new maneuvers, helping them to assess risk. Children will do what they can do, when they can do it.

Surfing: the ultimate balancing act.

During our summer program, we take advantage of our community of surfers to provide those in Kids' Club with new opportunities to practice balancing. Environmental activist and Patagonia surf ambassador Mary Osborne helps out as a surf instructor. She gives kids tips on paddling out and standing up on a surfboard.

right: Rell Sunn, circa 1994. Rell was the founder of Patagonia Surf. She was a true waterwoman who surfed, spearfished, freedived, and was said to be O'ahu's first female lifeguard. Her legacy lives on in her Menehune Surf Contest, which inspires children to love the ocean and surfing.
Spring Catalog 1995 — *John Russell*

We let young children take risks by climbing.

Climbing is driven by children's inborn desire to explore. Just as rolling over, sitting up, and pulling to stand have their own challenges and rewards, climbing provides a new perspective on the world and requires control and hand-eye coordination. Kids develop movement skills naturally as they play. When preschoolers climb, they practice bilateral integration, hand-eye coordination, muscular strength, and endurance. Respecting children means encouraging them to explore their capabilities. Safety is always foremost, but we do restrain ourselves from prematurely rescuing them, providing just a little assistance if truly necessary. Patagonia's roots are in climbing and in the mountains. It's in our DNA to watch our kids get an early start climbing.

Swinging stimulates the senses, provides exercise, and gives great joy.

Swings are a gleeful way to try to touch the sky, and they play an important role in the growing child's body by stimulating the senses and the vestibular system. When swinging, children exercise gross motor skills. Research shows that rocking and other movements through space help children's brains develop. At GPCDC, children must get onto swings on their own. Once they can get on independently, teachers give a single push, then explain and model how to pump legs to gain momentum.

Help children—especially girls—face their fears and complete tasks.

We are failing our girls. Parents are four times as likely to tell girls than boys to be careful (according to a 2015 study in *The Journal of Pediatric Psychology*). Girls are warned away from activities that hint of risk. Parents are more likely to assist their sons to face their fears with instructions on how to complete the task on their own. We need to teach both boys and girls the skills they need to be confident, responsible problem solvers and risk takers.

Jumping requires courage, leg strength, and an understanding of gravity.

Young children may choose to jump into the arms of a trusted caregiver before tackling the task alone. If a child feels confident enough to attempt a risky jump, we let them. Teachers stand by and give encouragement, offering physical assistance only if the situation becomes dangerous. We do not rescue children. When a child climbs with the intention of jumping, then decides it's not right, our teachers coach them. **Teachers say:** "You've climbed high. Do you want to jump down? If you don't, I will help you figure out how to climb down."

Mastering wheels is an important physical milestone.

Using scooters, pushcarts, tricycles, and bicycles are opportunities for problem solving and gives children practice with whole-body coordination—plus they can go on road trips with friends. In the photo to the right, our Kids' Club children take their bikes out for a self-powered field trip to the outskirts of town. Learning to ride a bicycle begins when toddlers practice maneuvering on and off. Eventually, they dis-cover how to scoot their feet, then off they go. Learning to steer, stop, and avoid traffic jams lasts a lifetime. We respect children's desire to learn in their own way and in their own time. If they want to spend all day getting on and off a scooter or sit all afternoon, motionless, on a tandem tricycle with a friend, that's fine.

— *GPCDC Practice* —

"Pump tires, not gas!"

In May each year, we celebrate the nationwide Bike to Work Day for an entire week, and in the days leading up to Bike to Work Week, colorful chalk drawings appear on the outdoor walkways at Patagonia's Ventura headquarters. There are pictures of bikes and phrases such as "Pump tires, not gas" and "Two wheels are better than four!" GPCDC hosts an event, and local police offer a bike safety clinic. One year, an employee brought an official racing bike and talked about its parts and gears. The kids also have their annual Bike Wash—it's all good, clean fun.

How can we best support fine motor development?

Chapter Ten: Working with Our Hands

During human evolution, increasingly complex use of tools evolved with thought and language—clearly, conscious thought, language, and manual dexterity are interrelated. It's the same for infants: The use of the hands parallels cognitive and language development. In fact, the very first action a baby learns is to reach a hand toward a loved one. The development of fine motor skills takes time and follows a predictable sequence. Using play, children develop dexterity that takes years to mature into refined ability. Given that developing the hands is such an important part of learning to function and think, our teachers provide many opportunities for children to practice.

"The hand enjoys a privileged status in the learning process, being not only a catalyst but an experiential focal point for the organization of the young child's perceptual, motor, cognitive, and creative world." — *Frank Wilson*

Mouthing is one of the earliest stages of fine motor development.

Because taste is the sense that develops first, infants grab objects and bring them straight to their mouths. This can be challenging to do without clocking oneself in the nose. Controlling the path from the hand to the mouth requires a good deal of fine motor skill. According to the National Center for Infants, Toddlers, and Families,

"By mouthing and handling objects as a baby—safely, of course—she becomes 'fluent' in ideas like side, edge, and corner. She doesn't have to 'rediscover' blocks each time she plays. This enables your child to automatically apply this knowledge to solve more and more complex problems, like how to build a block tower."

Reaching is an indicator of infants' development.

Like intrepid explorers eager to meet the world, babies' hands venture forth. Before infants can use their hands, they must develop the hand-eye coordination needed to grasp things. Newborns can't control their gaze, but as their vision gets clearer, they see objects and people they want. For example, in the photo above, an infant reaches for a little friend. Caregivers don't place objects in babies' hands, rather they put them close by so young infants can practice reaching. They provide items large enough for babies to hold but not too heavy, and only soft things at first. Infants must learn how to grasp and also how to let go of objects. Caregivers allow children to struggle through these challenging steps.

Babies must think and work hard to grasp and pick up objects.

Once infants figure out how to aim their hands accurately, they practice grasping. The simplest grasp uses the entire hand. It's challenging for infants to figure out how much arm or wrist movement is needed, how wide to spread the fingers, and the right time to close them.

Picking up an object with one hand is also tricky, and with two hands, it's doubly difficult. In order to be successful, the brain must be developed enough to tell the hands how to work together. Babies practice these skills over and over until they become second nature.

The pincer grasp indicates refined finger dexterity.

Like other areas of development, fine motor skills present themselves in stages. As babies become toddlers, they develop a pincer grasp, using the thumb and pointer finger—as the two-year-old in the photo above demonstrates. The pincer grasp is needed for opening containers, getting dressed, and holding a pencil, and it takes most of early childhood to strengthen and refine it. Teachers help children develop a stronger pincer grasp by providing opportunities to use it. Collecting small objects to place in a container and picking up finger foods or worms are motivating ways to practice.

Choose toys that help children practice using their hands.

Toys that require children to fit objects together not only strengthen the hand but refine hand-eye coordination. *Does this ball fit in this can? Does this block fit in this box? How do I get these shapes from this shape sorter into these holes?* As children become mobile and hone their fine motor skills, the environment offers increasingly complex opportunities for them to use their hands. Older children use all kinds of objects—balls, bead mazes, moving cars, bubble play, cars on tracks, and shape sorters—to improve fine motor skills and hand-eye coordination. The right toys at the right time engage children mentally and physically.

Constructing with linking blocks engages hands and minds.

Using small building bricks (think LEGOs) poses a particularly engaging fine motor challenge. As children's fine motor skills develop, they can use smaller and smaller building bricks, which are more challenging to fit together and pull apart. Children practice their pincer grasp when picking up the small pieces; they use precision to put them in place and hand strength to both snap them down and pull them apart.

Advance fine motor skills and develop dexterity with sticky tape.

Using tape precisely requires finger strength to pinch and pull it, and dexterity to cut or tear it. Children learn that if they don't handle tape carefully, it ends up stuck to itself, paper, and their hair and hands. Working with sticky tape can be frustrating, but it's valuable practice. Once children master using tape, it quickly becomes part of all kinds of play, as costumes, barriers, and the go-to for fixing anything broken. Although quite different from sticky tape, papier-mâché is a creative, messy way to practice fine motor skills. It also allows children to experience transformation as sodden paper dries and becomes solid sculpture.

Working with play dough helps children exercise hand muscles.

Using play dough and clay are the best fine motor activities for every age, because children grasp, pinch, pull, poke, roll, knead, and push it with open palms. Cookie cutters, rolling pins, scissors, straws, dull knives, cars, wooden meat tenderizers, and colanders are some of the tools teachers supply, along with play dough and clay, to help children develop a range of finger and hand dexterity.

Children become more independent as skills grow.

We emphasize self-reliance, so children refine their fine motor skills as they play, prepare for meals, and dress themselves. Teachers encourage children to dress themselves as appropriate for their age and skill. Toddlers can remove their socks and shoes. Three- and four-year-olds must at least try to put on socks, shoes, and zip their jackets before asking for help. Kids' Club children (ages five and up) are taught to tie their shoes.

We choose activities that hone hand-eye coordination and patience.

When children string beads or thread needles, they hone their hand-eye coordination skills and their patience. Infants and young toddlers begin learning these skills by pulling a rope through their hands or working with large wooden beads. Three- and four-year-olds practice lacing relatively small beads on yarn. Children of varying ages and abilities are exposed to different types of threading activities, but they all employ equal amounts of concentration.

Manipulating puzzle pieces requires dexterity and brain power.

Children use fine motor skills when working with puzzles, but they also use their minds. Puzzles tap into memory and problem-solving skills when children must remember that a piece that didn't fit in one place could now fit in another. Each puzzle piece is differently shaped, and children must focus on shape characteristics and apply what they've seen to complete the puzzle. Some children enjoy using strategic thinking to solve puzzles as fast as possible. Children work on puzzles independently and even struggle at times. Teachers observe and praise children for persistence and hard work, instead of stepping in and doing the work for them.

Children astound me with their inquisitive minds. The world is wide and mysterious to them, and as they piece together the puzzle of life, they ask 'Why?' ceaselessly. — *John C. Maxwell*

For advanced skills: scissors, knives, pens, and pencils.

Sophisticated fine motor skills mean new challenges. We foster purpose and responsibility by letting older children help prepare snacks with child-safe knives. Scissors strengthen all hand muscles and require complex hand-eye coordination. Sketching pictures, writing notes to friends, creating treasure maps: Children use drawing for both play and communication. Making marks on paper offers immediate feedback to children about their fine motor development. You will often find them day after day drawing the same circle, smiley face, or letter, delighting in their improved control.

Fine motor development apex: using tools to build and repair.

Children feel like grown-ups when using tools. Hammering, sawing, and drilling require dedicated focus and challenge children to exercise control. The tasks provide effective fine motor practice and foster confidence and creativity. We try to find authentic tasks for children to participate in, so when Kids' Club needed new garden boxes, the kids helped build them.

We taught our kids, and all their friends, to do home repairs with real tools, cook, sew, blacksmith, and to drive stick shift. Conversely, due to fears for their safety, most children now spend their time indoors in overscheduled, supervised lessons; competing in team sports; and having indoor, monitored play dates. —*Malinda Chouinard*

Were all instructors to realize that the quality of mental process, not the production of correct answers, is the measure of educative growth, something hardly less than a revolution in teaching would be worked.

—*John Dewey*

How does language spark creativity and problem solving to broaden horizons?

Chapter Eleven: Constructing Meaning

Language shapes thinking. Early childhood is the time when both inner and outer language develop, and how we speak to children influences their thinking for years to come. Our thoughts are limited or expanded by the concepts and words we know, and research indicates that without language, we can't think even simple ideas like: *The object is located left of the blue wall*. Often language that supports creativity, independence, and critical thinking isn't intuitive and requires adults to change how they speak to children.

Infants understand words first and speak later.

Although infants don't speak, they are born communicating. Crying is their first language. They also use nonverbal cues, which caregivers carefully observe in order to learn the unique language of each child. Babies comprehend words before they produce them, therefore we speak and use sign language with infants, knowing that if they don't understand already, they will soon.

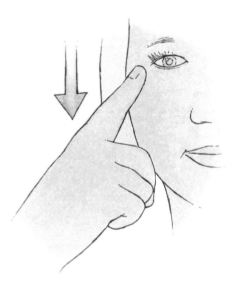

Sad

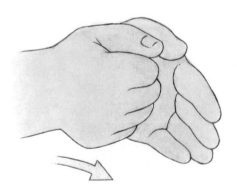

Wash

We speak not only to tell other people what we think, but to tell ourselves what we think. — *Oliver Sacks*

Before nursing, a mother says and signs "milk."

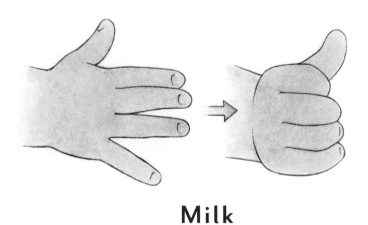

Milk

Sign language gives babies another way to communicate.

We teach infants American Sign Language (ASL) to give them a nonverbal form of expression. Being able to communicate needs and desires reduces frustration and strengthens the bond between caregiver and infant. We use an ASL dictionary to find unknown signs for words or concepts. We include the children in the process, so they understand that teachers—and all adults—don't know everything and are constantly learning, exploring, and evolving, too.

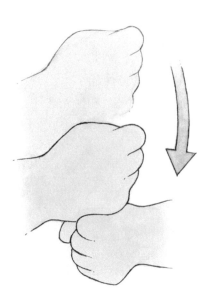

Work

An infant watches his father say and sign, "I am going to work."

Eat

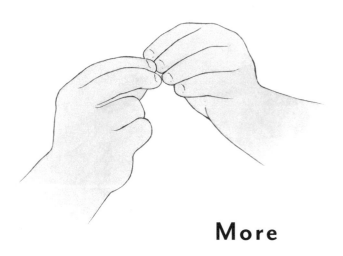

More

Given their dexterity and coordination, children attempt to mimic the signs adults model. Here a child creates his own version of the sign for "more."

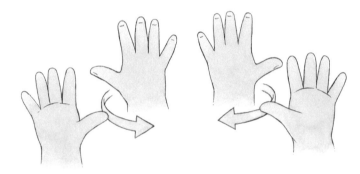

All Done

Sitting in the lap of his caregiver, an infant uses sign language to let everyone know that he's "all done" with his meal.

A toddler indicates she wants water, and the teacher responds in Spanish and ASL before handing her a pitcher of water to pour herself.

Water

Time

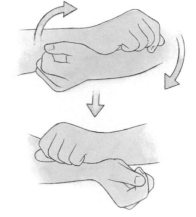

to
Change

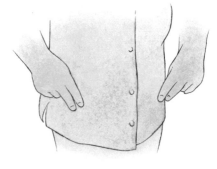

your
Diaper

As children get older and more skilled, teachers guide them toward ASL standard signs.

Problem solving is the foundation of learning.

John Dewey once said, "We only think when we are confronted by problems." If something doesn't challenge us, we've already mastered it. Children must have a positive attitude toward problems and possess a range of skills for solving them in order to thrive in learning environments. There are ways of thinking and speaking that teachers and parents can use to support children in becoming lifelong problem solvers.

Narration helps children complete challenging tasks.

One of the first ways that children use language to solve problems is by talking themselves through the steps of a task: "I need a block to finish my tower. This block is too short. I need a skinny one …" Initially, young children verbalize self-talk, but as children mature, self-talk is internalized. When teachers narrate how and why they are doing something, children internalize step-by-step thinking and use it to become independent problem solvers. **Teachers say:** "I'm looking for a green puzzle piece that will match this piece," or "I am trying to put these blocks back on the shelf, but they don't fit. Maybe I'll turn them sideways to see if they fit."

Appropriate challenges foster determination.

One way to create good problem solvers is to give children experiences that balance challenge and success. Theorist Lev Vygotsky called this the "zone of proximal development." It refers to the range of activities and skills that children are ready to learn. An infant will not be able to stack blocks, but she may be ready, given practice and encouragement, to crawl to that toy she's been eyeing.

Divergent thinking is linked to creativity.

Problem solving generally refers to doing what it takes to reach a specific goal: How can I place these blocks in a square? This is called convergent problem solving, and it's the primary focus of most education. But there's also divergent problem solving, which asks questions like: "How many uses, realistic and fanciful, can I find for a set of chairs?" Strong thinkers are proficient in both, yet most schools fail to promote divergent thinking. Young children are naturally divergent thinkers, but tend to score lower on divergent problem solving tests as they get older. We do what we can to promote both convergent and divergent thinking. These two-year-olds made a train out of chairs.

Good problem solvers know themselves and face challenges well.

In the 1960s, psychologist Walter Mischel placed marshmallows in front of four-year-olds. He told children that if they hadn't eaten the treat when he returned in fifteen minutes, he'd give them two marshmallows. Some children were able to wait, and others couldn't. For several years, Mischel followed the children's progress in school and learned that those who could delay gratification worked harder for future rewards and were more successful. These children could also recount to researchers their strategies for resisting the marshmallow. Children who strategize ways to cope with delayed rewards accomplish difficult tasks more successfully.

The self is not something ready-made, but something in continuous formation through choice of action.

— *John Dewey*

Children live and breathe stories.

Educator Vivian Paley once said that if you don't know your students' stories, then you don't really know your students. Young children live and breathe stories. Much of pretend play is storytelling in motion. An easy way to promote language development and early literacy is to fill children's lives with books. Reading to children not only connects them to their favorite stories, but it exposes them to vocabulary and print-knowledge. More recently, researchers also found that people who read fiction are more empathetic, because reading about the internal lives of others teaches us to consider people's thoughts and motivations.

Children play with reading and writing.

We incorporate reading and writing activities in fun, meaningful ways, because children experience the power of literacy by playing with it. Our indoor and outdoor classrooms are full of books of all sorts; children can interact with books on their own terms. Teachers read aloud to students, in both Spanish and English, and children create stories based on illustrations. Encouraging children to create their own stories empowers them as they develop reading skills, so teachers transcribe children's dictated stories to illustrate to them how words connect to their thoughts, feelings, and imaginations. In our dramatic play area, we have cookbooks and notepads that children use for pretend recipes and grocery lists.

Four-year-olds find letters everywhere.
Here, they spell out GPCDC.

Early literacy is about making language meaningful.

During the past few decades, the first-grade literacy curriculum has moved into kindergarten, and "educational" companies have marketed products that teach children to read at earlier ages. Despite years of research demonstrating no lasting benefit for early reading, the pressure on young children grows. We do not subscribe to the current trend. We do, however, know that preschool is an important time to build literacy skills. Good preschools make written language understandable and interesting, so that young children are motivated to read.

Children must be taught how to think, not what to think.

— *Margaret Mead*

296

Nursery rhymes and songs promote literacy.

There is evidence that when children practice rhyming, they learn to read more easily—perhaps because rhyming requires attention to the sounds that make up words. When children practice rhyming words, they practice skills needed to sound out unfamiliar words, and sounding out words is essential for beginning reading. Nursery rhymes and songs are fun and also help prepare children to read.

Spanish strengthens language skills.

We sing songs and read books aloud in Spanish, and each classroom has at least one teacher who's a native Spanish speaker and speaks it exclusively. Our center is located in the multilingual society of Southern California, where children either speak or encounter Spanish, so we speak Spanish in addition to English and sign language. The benefits of being able to speak, read, and write a second language include academic success and also the immeasurable benefit of being able to communicate and connect with those from other cultures. A 2015 study from the University of Chicago revealed that children who are exposed to a second language grow up to be better communicators because they have an easier time understanding the perspectives of others. In addition, young children might have an advantage when acquiring the sounds of language, which could result in better pronunciation.

One language sets you in a corridor for life. Two languages open every door along the way. — *Frank Smith*

Ricitos de Oro y los Tres Osos.

When children understand language, they acquire it. We find creative ways to help children understand the Spanish they hear. To make the second language comprehensible, we read and tell *Goldilocks and the Three Bears* in English to our students. Then our bilingual teachers present a play of the story in Spanish, *Ricitos de Oro y los Tres Osos*. The children know the story, so they understand much of the Spanish, and it strengthens their growing comprehension skills. Combining storytelling and second-language acquisition is a two for one.

— *Parent Story* —

Under Two and Using Three Languages

In the infant/toddler room, teachers model English, Spanish, and sign language. A rich literacy environment has an effect on young children. One day, while visiting my son, I observed this firsthand.

I sat on the floor in the classroom, and my son came over with a book he wanted me to read aloud. *Los Pollitos Dicen* is a favorite of his that's a story and a song with accompanying gestures and signs. I speak a little Spanish, so it wasn't a problem for me to read the story and sing the song in Spanish. Several times he wanted to turn the page, and I followed his lead, describing the pictures in Spanish, which he demonstrated he understood by asking questions in English. At one point, another child interrupted us, and I stopped reading. My son immediately signed *more* and said, "Mo, mo!"

Exposure to Spanish, sign language, and English through songs, stories, and daily routines has given my son the ability to understand and communicate more effectively.

How can we foster intellectual wonder in children?

Chapter Twelve: Testing Theories

Young children think differently than adults; their minds are inquisitive but aren't yet ready for fact-based learning. Often described as young scientists because of their innate curiosity and sense of wonder, kids excel at asking questions, developing theories, and experimenting. Maria Montessori noticed that their minds are inherently mathematical and that they are driven to classify and order reality. Our children build critical-thinking skills as they play. Teachers support them with good questions and environments that prompt kids to ask questions and form theories.

"Children have real understanding only of that which they invent themselves, and each time that we try to teach them something too quickly, we keep them from reinventing it themselves." — *Jean Piaget*

Open-ended questions encourage critical thinking.

Too often adults ask children questions they know the answer to: "I like your shoes. What color are they?" These questions underestimate and insult children's abilities. Children, even nonverbal ones, like to wonder, theorize, discuss, and explain. Asking genuine, open-ended questions builds trust between kids and adults and invites them to share their thoughts. **Teachers say:** "What would happen if ...? How are you going to do that? What are some different things you could do? What does this remind you of?"

Children explore chemistry through transformation.

Many chemistry experiments involve dangerous chemicals and reactions that are too abstract for young minds. However, children can explore chemical reactions safely when they cook, watch ice melt, or mix water with sand or dirt. When they can control the quantity of materials with various properties to make new substances, they develop an understanding of basic chemical transformation.

Children are scientists by nature.

Young children, unwittingly use the scientific method often while they play. They hypothesize: *I bet if I throw this ball very hard on the ground it will bounce over the gate*. They test their hypothesis and form new theories based on the results: *It didn't go over the gate. Maybe if I climb on something and bounce it, it will*. The following guidelines from *Developing Constructivist Early Childhood Curriculum* help inform our practices:

The child must be able to produce the phenomenon by his or her own actions. If the activity isn't hands-on, then children will not be able to test their ideas.

The child must be able to vary his or her own actions. If children aren't able to control variables, they will not be able to test their theory and get varying results. For example, if children are experimenting with force and gravity using ramps and balls, but the ramps are set up in a way that children can't alter the incline, they will not be able to see that the incline of a ramp affects the ball's speed.

The reaction of the object must be observable. As a chemistry experiment, many teachers combine baking soda and vinegar to form a frothy, bubbling mixture, which children love. However, it isn't a good example of early science curriculum. The particles responsible for the effect are invisible and too abstract for the young mind, so children don't take anything away from the experiment.

The reaction of the object must be immediate. It's hard for young children to comprehend cause and effect if a reaction takes place over a long period of time. It's easier to test theories that can be observed quickly.

Early physics is all about motion.

Children often create physics experiments in play: *How fast will this car go if I make the ramp this high?* Teachers facilitate deeper thinking by making observations and questioning children's theories. **Teachers say:** "I noticed that the car went faster down the ramp and it slowed down when it traveled up the next ramp. I wonder why that happened?" When children explain, either verbally or through physical action, teachers take note, ask follow-up questions, or share the theory with a larger group of children for discussion. They also change the materials to support further investigation.

By observing flora and fauna, young kids engage with biology.

It's sometimes difficult to test biological theories without doing harm: *I wonder what happens when I pull the legs off a beetle?* But naturalist Charles Darwin developed the scientific theory of evolution by combining his observations with those of farmers and botanists. Children will watch a turtle make its way across the ground and return to the same flower again and again. They continually theorize about the natural world. Engaging young children in discussions about their observations is a great way to create lifelong naturalists. **Teachers say:** "I wonder where that turtle is going? Do you think he likes the flower, and that's why he's crawling that way?"

Naturalist wonder.

We foster children's natural drive to explore nature by providing books about nature and animals and also giving them lots of time outdoors to explore. We often witness the benefits of encouraging children to be observant. In the photo on the left, when the child points to a bird illustration, the teacher says and signs, "bird," which the child mimics. Later in the day, while on the play yard, the child signs, "bird" as she notices crows flying overhead.

Playing with math concepts comes naturally.

It can be difficult to imagine how young children practice math when the subject brings to mind equations puzzled out on paper. However, when you consider that math is defined as "... the science of numbers, quantities, and shapes and the relations between them ..." you see that children often use math as they play. When they build, they play with shape and size. Hands-on activities prepare children for the more abstract mathematical work they'll be asked to do in the future.

The language of math sets up children for success.

Adults often shy away from using mathematical language with children. They readily offer scientific language or define difficult words in a book, but they rarely use math terms. The more we speak with children using math concepts, the more familiar they will be with the language of math they will encounter throughout their school careers.

Teachers say: "I see on this page that the caterpillar ate one apple, one pear, and ..."; "I wonder which pile has fewer shells?"; or "If I add a place for one more person to this table, there will be four people sitting here."

Kids develop math skills by exploring quantity.

When children make piles of objects, some bigger and some smaller, they begin to understand that there is more of one thing than another. This is the first step to understanding numbers more concretely. Teachers can help kids play with the idea of quantity through activities, questions, and observations. They can add a cash register and coins to a pretend-play area; buttons for sorting and adding to the block-building space; books that focus on quantity in the library; or a collection of shells, magnifying glasses, and boxes for sorting in the "science corner." Good questions and observations cue children into the mathematical nature of their play. **Teachers say:** "Which pile has more? I wonder if there are fewer red buttons than black ones?" or "It looks like these block towers have an equal amount of blocks."

Self-correcting activities offer good practice in math.

Much of the Montessori preschool curriculum is founded on activities that are self-correcting, meaning that children work on their own toward a goal that can't be completed unless they've followed the proper steps. This allows children to practice making mistakes and correcting them on their own. These types of activities, like puzzles, are also good practice for the kinds of math equations children will encounter in elementary school. We provide self-correcting materials as options during playtime. In the photo above, the goal is to have the same color clips on the bowl.

Kids say numerals before knowing that numbers show quantity.

One-to-one correspondence is the understanding that an individual object refers to a specific number. Children who haven't developed this skill will count by pointing randomly and reciting whatever numbers they know. Learning one-to-one correspondence is a developmental step that comes in the preschool years and can be fostered by object play. Often parents despair that their child won't be good at math because he or she can't count objects, but teachers encourage them not to worry since this skill comes with time.

Patterning teaches decision making.

Patterning is an important math skill because it's about connections and associations. It's the ability to predict a future outcome based on past experience. Patterning extends beyond math and teaches children to make informed life decisions. In order to pattern, children must classify and systematize: *What are the parts of the face, and how do they fit together?* or *How can I place the parts in a way that demonstrates similarities and differences?* We give kids materials that can be sorted by color, shape, size, or use and emphasize that there are no wrong ways to create patterns.

The process of drawing, painting, or constructing is a complex one in which children bring together diverse elements of their experience to make a new and meaningful whole. In the process of selecting, interpreting, and reforming these elements, children have given us more than a picture or a sculpture; they have given us a part of themselves: how they think, feel, and see.

— *Lowenfeld and Brittain*

Kids numbering in English have a harder time.

Children mastering numbering are learning to count and recognize written numbers. Interestingly, English-speaking children have a difficult task, because English doesn't have consistent rules about numbers. Think of the teens: 10, 11, and 12 do not have the word *teen*, like the rest of the sequence. In Chinese, the spoken words for numbers reflect the mathematical system, so 21 translates into *two tens plus one*. The Chinese language reflects the pattern of numbers—in English, this isn't the case. In the photos above, children use apples as the standard of measure, and then count to find out how tall they are in apples.

Investigating space develops geometric reasoning.

Children experiment with the properties of shape, size, and space when they play with puzzles and building bricks, cut paper and reorder the pieces, or use toys such as shape sorters. All of these activities are the hands-on precursors to geometry.

Balancing a sense of wonder with a few rules.

We know that much of children's future schooling will require working well with others and, at times, following directions and rules of one kind or another. We want our children to be well-prepared, so we give them many opportunities to practice working in groups and following directions and rules, which allows these skills to develop.

Following directions requires sequential thinking, so teachers infuse their language with words that help children track order. **Teachers say:** "First, we put the blocks away on the shelf. Then we line up and go to the Trolley Yard."

In our lessons and activities, we try to think outside of the box. We strive to find new, exciting ways to connect children authentically with the world of science and math. — *Nicole Marie*

Passion is lifted from the earth itself by the muddy hands of the young; it travels along grass-stained sleeves to the heart. If we are going to save environmentalism and the environment, we must also save an endangered indicator species: the child in nature.

— *Richard Louv*

How can we inspire children to be stewards of the planet?

Chapter Thirteen: Raising the Next Generation

We want children to love nature so that they protect it in the future. To do that, children must have time to play outside, communing with plants and relating to the heroic march of ants. Being in nature is just plain good for children and adults. In 2015, a Stanford University study determined that walking outdoors in a park for one hour made the test subjects happier than walking for an hour in a city. A recent study done in Amsterdam found that even images of natural settings can help students relax and improve their abilities in school. One of the scientists involved mused, "Just imagine the effect of real trees." Not only do children benefit from nature, but nature benefits from children.

"I only went out for a walk and finally concluded to stay out till sundown, for going out, I found, was really going in." — *John Muir*

"A hunger for trees ..."

A UNESCO survey of children's needs found that no matter where a child lived—in America or Australia; Poland or Borneo; in city, suburb or rural village—there was an outspoken and universal "hunger for trees." It is a poignant reminder that children's relationship with nature is a keen and very natural one, and that a connection to the natural world is as essential to their lives as food and love.

The bond between kids and nature, especially our precious, ever-shrinking, truly wild places, is mutually beneficial. From toddling after a sand crab on the beach to helping prepare camp in the high country, kids experience the natural world with all senses. Blessed with what Albert Einstein called "holy curiosity" (he warned adults never to lose it), kids quite simply feel the planet underneath them.

In return, wilderness offers healthy nutrients, such as fresh air; space and beauty; and the vital experiences of discovery, solitude, silence. It provides valuable lessons about the interdependence of all life and about toughness and self-reliance, sensitivity, and physical strength. These lessons are as important as learning to read, as satisfying as spreading across a canvas the very blue you saw in your mind. The more kids feel a part of the natural world around them, the greater concern they will have for its well-being as they grow.

We believe the child-nature bond needs all the help it can get. It's up to us to see to it that children don't go tree hungry, that they have wild places and the opportunities to be in them. Once they do, they will amaze us with their caring. They need not wait to grow up to be involved; part of becoming a responsible adult is having a sense of responsibility for the environment as a child. Their own well-being depends on it.

Spring Catalog 1990 — *Rick Graetz*

Kids thrive outdoors.

We don't need research to tell us that spending time outdoors is good for us. However, we love that research now supports what we've known for a long time. There is growing evidence that spending time in natural environments positively affects children. When children spend time in nature, they are happier, calmer, and more focused.

Our forefathers were in daily contact with their environment. Even in the last 50 years there have been dramatic changes. There is too little opportunity today for youngsters to dam up a stream, dig a tunnel to China, or build a tree house. The complete involvement of oneself in a project of purely physical, sensory nature is rapidly disappearing. Possibly the greater interest in camping, hiking, and skiing is a result of the urge to experience the senses more fully.

— *Lowenfeld and Brittain*

Nature is the ultimate sensory experience.

Children at GPCDC spend more than half their time outdoors in play spaces that are far from wild but which offer trees, rocks, dirt, and water—we simulate nature as best we can. There are places to climb and ever-changing, thought-provoking areas to explore. No indoor environment, toy, or technology rivals the unpredictability of nature.

When children need to run, jump, and climb, the best challenge is a landscape of grasses, rocks, and fallen trees. For quiet moments, turning over a rock reveals a diverse, alive ecosystem. We currently can't provide untamed nature at GPCDC, but we wholeheartedly believe that wild landscapes are unsurpassed at engaging children.

Playing outside prepares children for life.

In Scandinavian countries, researchers found that children who play in natural landscapes tested better in motor development compared to those who play on flat playgrounds. School-age children who are asked to focus for longer periods of time need outdoor play to support classroom learning. According to the American Institutes for Research, "Studies in California and across the United States showed that schools that used outdoor classrooms and other forms of nature-based experiential education saw significant student gains in social studies, science, language arts, and math."

— *GPCDC Practice* —

Outdoor Classroom

To deepen our understanding of how to support children's relationship to the outdoors, our staff are trained and certified by the Outdoor Classroom Project. You can find GPCDC on the Outdoor Classroom Project website (outdoorclassroomproject.org) as a model for this kind of learning.

Those who take inspiration from this program follow these tenets:

Most activities that can be done indoors can be done outdoors. Some activities occur best outdoors; some can only occur outdoors.

Children spend substantial periods of time outside, and it is easy and safe for them to get there; they are free to move easily between the indoors and outdoors.

There is a full range of activities for children, including many activities that are traditionally thought of as indoor activities.

The outdoor space offers a balance of areas for active and less-active play.

While outside, children frequently have the opportunity to initiate their own learning experiences and activities, with appropriate materials for them to use as they wish.

The outdoor curriculum evolves from and changes with children's changing needs and interests.

Children experience nature in as many ways as possible.

Any play yard can be filled with nature.

Our child-care center weaves between the buildings of our Ventura headquarters; it's not bordered by pristine forest. To make our play areas resemble green spaces, we plant trees, encourage native plants and animals, and grow vines on many of our fences. On the chain-link fences where we can't grow vines, we mask them with indoor-outdoor acrylic fabric printed with a design that resembles leaves. The children use the leafy backdrop as scenery for pretend play. In addition, our highly trained staff has found ways to bring the outdoors to life each day with surprise activities or objects—animal costumes, instruments, shells, magnifying glasses, pine cones, and paint. The photo to the right is a good example of this. Teachers have hidden an object in the wooden box, which has a single, small opening. They ask children to guess what's inside and also to use their senses to learn as much as they can without removing the object. **Teachers say:** "What can you see? What does it feel like? Does it make a sound?" After the object is revealed, children talk about the process of guessing and investigating to learn about an unknown object.

Those who contemplate the beauty of the earth find reserves of strength that will endure as long as life lasts. — *Rachel Carson*

Children who garden learn about the cycles of life.

Gardens connect children to the natural world. Our children plant, water, weed, harvest, and eat fresh fruits and vegetables all year long. They plunge their fingers into fresh soil, watch flowers transform into fruit, gingerly pluck berries and savor the sweet juices. They become emotionally attached to the plants, cheer on new growth, and wonder what's gone wrong when a plant doesn't thrive. Their day-to-day relationship with the garden fosters empathy toward the natural world, which blossoms into a desire to protect life.

Water conservation as a way of life.

Given that we reside in sunny-yet-drought-prone Southern California, we take water conservation seriously—and ask children to take it seriously as well. All ages reuse leftover water from snack and lunchtime to water the gardens. We discuss with older children how to save water in the outdoor areas. In order to save water, we've implemented these policies on our play yards. The "dog licks" that provide water for sand play are turned off between 11:30 a.m. and 4:30 p.m. Our water pump is a special activity that's used only once a month. In our messy kitchen area, a clear jug with a spigot is filled only once a day. As children use water, they can see the level dropping and monitor their consumption and conservation. And when it rains, GPCDC kids splash in the mud, dance, cheer, and chant, "The plants are drinking and happy!"

Anything else you're interested in is not going to happen if you can't breathe the air and drink the water. Don't sit this one out. Do something. You are by accident of fate alive at an absolutely critical moment in the history of our planet. *— Carl Sagan*

Connection with animals builds empathy.

In the same way gardening builds empathy with plants, positive inter-action with animals creates animal lovers. Watching animals eat, play, and sleep, children see that animal lives are filled with similar routines and concerns as human lives. The more experience children have with animals, the happier children feel and the more likely they are to grow up as advocates for animals' habitats. Our guinea pig, Butterscotch,

calls GPCDC home. Children exercise care when handling him and practice observation skills to determine when and how much to feed him. Teachers build children's empathy by initiating open-ended dis-cussions about Butterscotch's experiences. On long weekends, a lucky GPCDC family takes him home. Children delight in talking with their classmates about what Butterscotch did over the weekend.

Some people talk to animals.
Not very many listen, though.
That's the problem. — *Benjamin Hoff*

There is nothing in a caterpillar that tells you it's going to be a **butterfly.** — *Buckminster Fuller*

Insects are animals too.

Teachers coach children to interact gently with all insects, instilling respect for the life of every creature. We observe the daily habits of bees, ants, and other bugs; and children share news of their discoveries of spiderwebs, anthills, and wasp nests. Children learn about beneficial insects and worms firsthand by helping to release them into their gardens. Our campus is a certified monarch butterfly habitat, so in every garden we plant milkweed, a monarch caterpillar's only food. We use our environment to bolster dwindling populations of butterflies and give children the opportunity to observe all stages of the monarch's life cycle.

Children can teach parents environmental practices.

We not only build relationships with nature by giving children lots of time and experiences outdoors, but we also incorporate recycling, composting, and water reuse. Children grow up doing these things as second nature. They bring these practices home and often instigate change in their households. Every age group composts discarded food. Children regularly carry food scraps to worm bins and compost piles and can watch their food scraps turn to soil. The soil is then used in the gardens, which children eat from and then compost any leftover scraps. GPCDC children are often more familiar with zero-waste processes and practices than many adults.

Education's proper use is to enable citizens to live lives that are economically, politically, socially, and culturally responsible.

A proper education enables young people to put their lives in order, which means knowing what things are more important than other things; it means putting first things first. *— Wendell Berry*

Learning where our food comes from.

Caring for gardens, picking fruits and vegetables, and churning butter—all these tasks help children understand where their food comes from. As one child said, "We know our food is real because we pull it right out of the ground." We encourage parents to avoid bringing cake to the center to celebrate their child's birthday and opt instead for activities—such as pressing cider or making carrot juice— that encourage children to eat healthy foods and make celebrations about social experiences rather than sugary treats. When children take apples and place them in a cider press, they can see, touch, smell, and taste the process of whole apples being transformed into cider.

Our extended community offers even more experiences.

Children connect with nature by going on field trips. We find as many ways as we can to introduce children to the natural world. Our preschoolers visit the nearby county fair, which is within walking distance—teachers take them there in multi-child wagons. School-age children travel farther afield to the Museum of Ventura County, the Santa Barbara Zoo, and the Santa Barbara Museum of Natural History, which has its Sea Center at Stearns Wharf. Everyone enjoys the beach and local parks.

GPCDC kids visit the Turtle Conservancy in Ojai, California. The conservancy's central goal is to protect the habitat of the most endangered turtles and tortoises in the world. It also manages a propagation center that is successfully breeding some of these threatened species—but habitat remains the issue for their survival. School children are invited to visit. The kids then do their own fund-raisers to support the program.

For more effective education reform, teachers should free kids from the classroom.

— *Richard Louv*

Parents and kids volunteer together.

We celebrate the life and work of Martin Luther King Jr. by encouraging employees to spend MLK Day volunteering with nonprofit groups. Patagonia pays employees for their time. In past years, employees helped clear an area in the Sierras overtaken by invasive plants. Some of our school-age children worked alongside their parents planting native trees. We recently helped out the Ojai Valley Land Conservancy in a similar way by removing non-native plant species and planting native ones.

The most effective field trips are to places where children can return on a regular basis. For example, our Kids' Club children bike to Foster Park. Returning week after week, they become intimate with the land. They notice changes, acorns falling and flowers blooming. Their relationship to the place is multilayered, rooted in many experiences through time.

He who plants a tree, plants a hope. — *Lucy Larcom*

left: Fall Catalog 1994 — *Andy Van Herick* *top right:* Spring Catalog 1994 — *Sandra Miller*

We strive for full immersion field trips.

Children's thoughts, feelings, and senses are intertwined and connected to the places they live and visit. When our children go out into the world, we ask ourselves how can we safely give them the opportunity to interact as fully as possible? We want them to get sand between their toes, run on uneven surfaces, and feel chilly wind on their faces. We want them to feel free. This is how life, vitality, and meaning are infused into our program.

Beach cleanup: A dirty job, and kids can do it.

Do we want our kids to play on trash-littered beaches? Sometimes kids are the most effective activists. Future stewards of the Earth must hone their skills, so our older children walk to the local surf break and collect trash.

But I arise in the morning torn between a desire to improve the world and a desire to enjoy the world. — E. B. White

Kids are part of the solution.

Cleaning beaches, smashing cans, composting food scraps—these activities are not hard work for children. They're fun. Kids love to contribute in meaningful ways, so we give them opportunities to pitch in daily. A love for nature, and the disposition to go the extra mile to protect it, is built over time and reinforced by small, consistent, and meaningful moments.

Our children remind us of our responsibilities to the planet.

Patagonia has always been committed to finding environmental solutions. Having on-site child care lets us watch children play from the windows of our offices and fuels our urgency to improve our business processes. When our children shout with delight when harvesting a hidden carrot or toss a pile of autumn leaves into the air, they remind us that nature is wondrous and worth protecting for future generations—our children's children and beyond.

Where are we going from here?

Anita Garaway-Furtaw arrived at Patagonia in 1985 with a vision: Child care was not babysitting. Her goal was to create a child-care center with a focus on respect and support for children in an atmosphere that nurtures their innate sense of wonder.

Anita's concept rejected the growing, and enduring, fascination with computer technology—she dismissed the VHS videotape player her first week at GPCDC. She advocated for creative play, during which children learn social skills. She believed in teaching qualities, such as empathy and teamwork, that foster social interaction. Patagonia children and their working parents flourished in this environment. Today, many GPCDC graduates work at Patagonia. These employees were once in our infant and preschool programs and are the legacy of the center's long history (in some cases, their own children are now in the program).

Over time, the curriculum has grown to include bilingual immersion, sign language, art, music, and the Outdoor Classroom. In these settings, our children develop social and creative skills and the confidence they need to navigate the world as social animals.

Looking ahead to GPCDC's next three decades, we're inspired by programs and schools that give children unstructured time to play and learn in nature.

left: Fall Catalog 1992 — *Yvon Chouinard*

"Go outside and play. Get some sunshine."

That was the healthy norm 30 years ago. Our kids and their friends played freely around Patagonia's office building after school. In the summer, they were in the forest, building a log raft or a nesting box for birds. Their only rule was: Stay together within range of being called home for dinner. Yvon insisted that children figure things out for themselves, by spending hours each day outside. We taught our kids, and their friends, to do home repairs with real tools, cook, sew, blacksmith, and drive stick shift.

Conversely, due to safety fears, most children spend their time indoors participating in tightly scheduled, supervised lessons and team sports and in closely monitored play dates. Parents even demand that preschools teach age-inappropriate, curiosity-stifling academics. Journalist Alison Flood reveals that "'There is a shocking, proven connection between the decline in natural play and the decline in children's wellbeing' ... Research found that a generation ago, 40% of children regularly played in natural areas, compared to 10% today, with a further 40% never playing outdoors. 'Obesity, anti-social behavior, friendlessness, and fear are the known consequences.'"

School structures should be flexible and put children's needs first; plans and methods must evolve so as not to single out children to a social disadvantage. Some schools have unrealistic, unhealthy expectations, including keeping four-year-olds at desks and penalizing those who cannot sit still—these schools create demoralized students.

Our initial goal for this book was to promote corporate-sponsored, on-site child care by illustrating with photos the practices at GPCDC. We wanted to show how children, parents, and the workplace benefit from quality child care, which most importantly gives nursing mothers access to their babies throughout the workday. We also wanted to emphasize how crucial it is to develop social and physical skills before academics.

As we reviewed successful best practices for this book, we saw the opportunity to advocate for quality child care and to amplify what is best in our practices. As toddlers cease nursing and become toilet trained, three-year-olds require increasing opportunities to develop their creativity, social, and sensory perception. As it was when we and our grandparents were all children, unstructured outdoor play is still the most stimulating and healthy place for children.

Space is always a problem for companies, but on-site infant and preschool child care remain essential. We struggle with growth—we're adding a third infant classroom. But as our five-year-olds graduate to community kindergartens, it is our colleagues who struggle. They lament that most, if not all, private and public kindergarten programs substitute outdoor time with academics, computer-based learning, and preparation for standardized tests. Rather than acquiesce to the trend toward inappropriately academic curricula, we are making plans to develop kindergarten and after-school programs that emphasize nature and being outside.

Outdoor, nature-based forest schooling has grown more appealing in direct proportion to children's loss of nature. Forest schools, also called nature schools, are not new. Leslie Paul founded the Woodcraft Folk in 1925, inspired by the earlier work of Susan Isaacs. "Whole days in

woodlands learning personal, social, and technical skills provides natural self-regulated opportunities to develop confidence through hands-on learning." This is in stark contrast to the majority of America's children who are increasingly desk-bound, bereft of physical education, art, music, and free time to think and to enjoy their families. Research shows that stimulation for the imagination is best and least expensively done in nature.

Our parents and grandparents were raised outside and had unstructured free time. However, our children are with us at work, not running around the farm. So our talented staff is making plans for new programs; their guiding vision is the ideal of being raised outside.

As our Outdoor School program develops more focus on the outdoors and our seven-year-olds graduate to community schools, we strengthen our resolve for all children to thrive in quality environments. We advocate to revive unstructured outdoor time for all children, in all schools, as the key to quality education.

This is not the time for Americans to lose their creativity, hand-eye coordination, balance, physical strength, and mental clarity. Now and into the future, against the growing pressure toward convergent thinking, we will adopt opportunities to "turn around and take a step forward" with our free-range children.

above: Spring Catalog 1988 — *Yvon Chouinard* The Future

Wild landscapes are especially good for children because their senses are engaged on every level. When children need to run, jump, and climb, the best challenge is a landscape full of grasses, rocks, and fallen trees. For quieter moments, turning over a rock reveals a miniature ecosystem diverse and alive. No toy, technology, or indoor environment can rival the unpredictability of nature.

— *Nicole Marie*

What every kid should be able to do by age 16.

— *Audrey Sutherland* —

Audrey Sutherland was an accomplished writer and waterwoman. She was also a mother and, 40 years ago, wrote impressive goals for her children, which have come to us via her list "What every kid should be able to do by age 16." Our children need skills and confidence to be competent adults, and Audrey's list is an important point of comparison for us today.

Swim 400 yards easily

Do dishes in a strange house, and your own

Cook a simple meal

See work to be done and do it

Care for tools and put them away after use

Splice or put a fixture on an electric cord

Know basic information about five careers that suit you

Volunteer to work for a month in each of those fields

Clean a paintbrush after use

Change a diaper, and a tire

Listen to an adult talk with interest and empathy

Take initiative and responsibility for school work and home chores

Dance with any age

Clean a fish and dress a chicken

Drive a car with skill and sanity

Know and take responsibility for sexual conception and protection when needed

Know the basic five of first aid: restore breathing and heartbeat, control bleeding, dilute poisons, immobilize fractures, treat for shock

Write a business letter

Use the family income to pay all bills and necessities for two months

Know basic auto mechanics and simple repair

Find your way across a strange city using public transportation

Be happy and comfortable alone for 10 days, 10 miles from the nearest other person

Save someone drowning using available equipment

Find a paying job and hold it for a month

Read at a tenth grade level

Read a topographic map and a chart

Handle a boat safely and competently (canoe, kayak, skiff, sailboat)

Operate a sewing machine and mend your own clothes

Do your own laundry

Spring Catalog 1992 — *Didier Givois*

These are the people who made the *Family Business* book and videos happen.

Malinda Chouinard
Patagonia and GPCDC
Co-Founder

Rose Marcario
Patagonia CEO

Kristine McDivitt Tompkins
Patagonia Co-Founder and
Former CEO

Cameron Tambakis
Photo Editor

Jennifer Ridgeway
GPCDC Co-Founder,
Art Director, Photo Editor

Carin Knutson
Managing Editor

Nicole Marie
Lead Writer

Kyle Sparks
Photographer

Carissa Tudor
Family Business Filmmaker

Alannah Zurovski
Writer and
GPCDC Teacher

Anita Garaway-Furtaw
GPCDC Director
(1985–2016)

Tommee McMakin
Writer and
Former GPCDC Teacher

Mary Jo Thomas
Senior Graphic Designer

Hilary McLeod
Project Manager

Karla Olson
Director of Patagonia Books

Whitney Clapper
Global Brand Marketing Manager

Jordan Damron
Production Artist

Rafael Dunn
Production Manager

We would like to thankfully acknowledge everyone who has assisted with the creation of this book, most importantly the children, their parents, and the teachers.

GREAT PACIFIC CHILD DEVELOPMENT CENTER
DIRECTORS, TEACHERS, AND STAFF

Anita Garaway-Furtaw, Sheryl Shushan, Maureen McCarthy Vasquez, Thelma Aviles, Susan Welbourn, Dona Folk, Alannah Zurovski, Dianna Alvarado, Nicolette Walker Itza, Heather Van Vorst, Janet Abernathy, Marin Pearce, Lori Cloutier, Cristina Gavia, Kelsey Pronovost, Christina Stewart, Kat Cryer, Ana DeLeon, Denise Duran, Megan Fronterhouse, Melissa DeLaRosa, Federica Rangel, Dana Waslosky, Dania Martinez, Courtney Checky, Lisa De Lara, Mary Buonocore, Elyse Levine, Lorraine Walter, Nancy Neilan, Allena Dills, Hailey King, Jessica Schulte, Emily Treischel

PHOTOGRAPHERS

Kyle Sparks, our staff photographer, took 300 of the 500 photos published in this book. Without him, this book would not have been possible.

We have also included spontaneous moments captured by our Great Pacific Child Development Center teachers, past and present.

In addition, we have included photographs by Jay Tayag, Michael K. Nichols, Gary Regester, Somira Sao, Ted Tambakis, Peter Bohler/ Redux, Mandel Ngan/Getty Images, Tony Jessen, Yvon Chouinard, Rick Ridgeway, Tim Davis, Dwight Tudor, Dylan Johnson, Billie Jan Houston, Hilary McLeod, Terri Laine, and Karen Frishman. If a photograph was published in one of our Patagonia catalogs, we cite the photographer on the page.

PHOTO ARCHIVISTS

Karen Bednorz, Sus Corez

WRITERS

Nora Gallagher, Joanne Dornan, Carissa Ridgeway Tudor, Jasin Nazim, Adam Fetcher, Vincent Stanley, Susanne Pennoyer, Carol Flanagan, Kit Cossart

PRODUCTION

Natausha Greenblott, Monique Martinez, our friends at Image Source

EDITORIAL

Laurie Gibson, Doug Adrianson, April Bailey, John Dutton, Sarah Hartigan, L. D. Porter

REVIEWERS

Claire Chouinard, Rose Marcario, Kris Tompkins, Nora Gallagher, Rick Ridgeway, Bill Boland, Hilary Dessouky, Anita Garaway-Furtaw, Sheryl Shushan, Thelma Aviles, Adam Fetcher, Dean Carter, Susanne Pennoyer, Carissa Ridgeway Tudor, Eugénie Frerichs, Michael Leon, Jane Sievert, Mary Heebner, Caroline Zimmerman, Sonia Moore, Lisa Sander, Robert Tadlock, Traci Escamilla

LOVING THANKS

To the memory of Helen and Jordan Pennoyer, Jeff Chouinard, Rell Sunn, Tex Bossier, Young Sunwoo, Clova Campbell, Tom Dixon, and Dorene Frost, whose photographs we used as an integral part of our history.

PART ONE

INTRODUCTION

PG. 9 In almost two-thirds of married-couple families, both parents work. In single-parent families, the percentage of working parents is even higher. Kim Parker and Wendy Wang, "Modern Parenthood: Roles of Moms and Dads Converge as They Balance Work and Family," Pew Research Center (March 14, 2013): accessed April 13, 2016, http://www.pewsocialtrends.org/2013/03/14/modern-parenthood-roles-of-moms-and-dads-converge-as-they-balance-work-and-family/.

WEIGHING THE BUSINESS CASE

PG. 12 The poet Maya Angelou said, "When you know better, you do better." Interview by Oprah Winfrey, October 2011. "The Powerful Lesson Maya Angelou Taught Oprah," Accessed April 13, 2015, http://www.oprah.com/oprahs-lifeclass/The-Powerful-Lesson-Maya-Angelou-Taught-Oprah-Video.

PG. 12 Collectively, we American business leaders provide paid family leave to just 11 percent of U.S. workers. The Council of Economic Advisers, "The Economics of Paid and Unpaid Leave," Executive Office of the President of the United States, Council of Economic Advisers (June 2014): accessed April 13, 2016, https://www.whitehouse.gov/sites/default/files/docs/leave_report_final.pdf.

PG. 12 As of April 2016, only three states and the District of Columbia offer paid family leave: California, New Jersey, and Rhode Island. Lisa Guerin, "Paid Family Leave in California, New Jersey, Rhode Island, Washington, and the District of Columbia:" accessed April 16, 2016, http://www.nolo.com/legal-encyclopedia/paid-family-leave-states-29854.html

PG. 12 Tax Benefits–Costs Recouped: 50%. Title 26–Internal Revenue Code Section 45F, "Employer-Provided Child Care Credit." Authenticated U.S. Government Information, 2016: accessed April 16, 2016, https://www.gpo.gov/fdsys/pkg/USCODE-2012-title26/pdf/USCODE-2012-title26-subtitleA-chap1-subchapA-partIV-subpartD-sec45F.pdf.

– As of publication, costs after revenues (tuition fees) for running Patagonia's child development center are approximately $1,000,000. With a yearly tax deduction of $150,000, and a second deduction of 35 percent of costs (35% X $1,000,000 = $350,000), that's a total of $500,000 in costs recouped, or 50 percent.

PG. 12 Employee Retention–Costs Recouped 30%

–To estimate the cost reductions due to on-site child care, we estimated the additional turnover we would have if we did not have an on-site child-care center and then estimated the cost of that turnover. This took three steps: calculating the cost of turnover, calculating the effect of on-site child care on turnover, and multiplying the cost of turnover by the expected reduction in turnover.

A review of the literature suggested turnover costs for nonmanagers in most companies is approximately 35 percent of salary, with 125 percent for managers, and 200 percent for directors and above.

To apply this to our company, we needed to break it into two stages: those who would resign right after maternity leave and those who would resign at any time after.

Right after childbirth: Between 20 and 35 percent of mothers do not return to work after birth and maternity leave; we took a middle estimate of 25 percent for the estimated expected turnover rate for this group. Over the past five years at Patagonia's headquarters, no mother has resigned due to maternity. Looking at the average number of maternity leaves we have in a year, their expected turnover costs (using their average salaries and the estimates of turnover cost above), and multiplying that by a 25 percent industry average turnover rate, we estimate we would have $160,500 in turnover costs if we did not have a child-care center.

Parents of children ages four months to six years: Comparing turnover over the past five years, we found that parents with a child in our program had a turnover rate approximately 25 percent less than our general population. Looking at the mix of levels and wages of employees with children in the program, calculating the expected cost of turnover–if that group acted like our general population–and then reducing that by 25 percent, expecting that they follow the historical trend of reduced turnover, we estimate that we are avoiding a turnover cost of approximately $150,000.

Adding these two together, we can estimate about $310,000 in costs is avoided every year. For a program that costs approximately $1,000,000, that is approximately a 30 percent of costs.

– Karlyn Borysenko, "What Was Management Thinking? The High Cost of Employee Turnover," Talent Management (April 22, 2015): accessed April 20, 2016. http://www.eremedia.com/tlnt/what-was-leadership-thinking-the-shockingly-high-cost-of-employee-turnover/.

– Wayne F. Cascio and John W. Boudreau, *Investing in People: Financial Impact of Human Resource Initiatives.* (Upper Saddle River, NJ: FT Press, 2008).

– Riane Eisler, *The Real Wealth of Nations: Creating a Caring Economics.* BK Currents. (San Francisco: Berrett-Koehler Publishers, 2008).

– Heather Boushey and Sarah Jane Glynn, "There Are Significant Business Costs to Replacing Employees," Center for American Progress (November 16, 2012): accessed April 20, 2016, https://www.americanprogress.org/wp-content/uploads/2012/11/CostofTurnover.pdf.

– Sylvia Anne Hewlett and Cynthia Buck Luce, "Off-Ramps and On-Ramps: Keeping Talented Women on the Road to Success," *Harvard Business Review* (March 2005): https://hbr.org/2005/03/off-ramps-and-on-ramps-keeping-talented-women-on-the-road-to-success.

– "Women Matter: Female Leadership, a Competitive Edge for the Future," McKinsey & Company (2008): accessed April 20, 2016. http://www.mckinsey.com/~/media/McKinsey/dotcom/client_service/Organization/PDFs/Women_matter_oct2008_english.ashx.

– Eileen Appelbaum and Ruth Milkman, "Achieving a Workable Balance: New Jersey Employers' Experiences Managing Employee Leaves and Turnover," (New Brunswick: Rutgers, n.d.).

– "Paid Leave," National Partnership for Women and Families (2016): accessed April 20, 2016, http://www.nationalpartnership.org/issues/work-family/paid-leave.html.

– National Partnership for Women and Families, "Women Leaving and Re-Entering The Workforce," *Catalyst* (March 28, 2013): accessed April 20, 2016. http://www.catalyst.org/knowledge/women-leaving-and-re-entering-workforce.

PG. 12 Employee Engagement–Costs recouped: 11%

–To estimate the effect of employee engagement due to on-site child care, we estimated the effect of on-site child care on engagement of parents who use the program, and then multiplied that by the estimated effect of a parents' engagement on the company's financial performance.

A Bright Horizons study of several thousand parents in a range of workplaces found that respondents with access to on-site child care answered on average 15-20 percent more positively to the questions used to gauge employee engagement. Studies by Gallup and Towers Perrin estimated a 0.12 to 0.14 percent increase in financial performance from every 1 percent increase in performance. That's a pretty small percentage, but when we are talking about multimillion-dollar companies, those numbers get big fast.

Taking the low end of those numbers to be conservative, multiplying that by the proportion of the headquarters employees who use our child-care center (which makes the conservative assumption that only users of the program have an engagement effect and that these typically high-level employees have as much effect on company performance as any other employee) and multiplying that by our net income at the time of publication, we estimate approximately $110,000 in income due to increased engagement, which works out to be approximately 11 percent of costs.

left: Spring Catalog 1996 — *Jim Russi*

Fall Catalog 1991 — *Yvon Chouinard*

—Lucy English and Jaime Ladge. "Enhanced Employee Health, Well-Being, and Engagement through Dependent Care Supports," Bright Horizons: accessed April 22, 2016, http://www.brighthorizons.com/email_images/webinar_06232010/enhanced_webinar_06232010.pdf.

PG. 13 **People don't have to choose between paying the bills and seeing their kids shine in the class play. And that means that that worker will do whatever it takes to help the company the next time out because they know that Rose and others at the very top are looking out for them.** Corey Simpson, "Kids: Our Best Product—Participating in the Champions of Change for Working Families Event at the White House" Patagonia Works: accessed May 12, 2016, http://www.patagoniaworks.com/press/2015/4/16/kids-our-best-product-participating-in-the-champions-of-change-for-working-families-event-at-the-white-house.

PG. 14 **JPMorgan Chase Bank, N.A., has estimated returns of 115 percent for its child-care program ...;** W. F. Cascio and John W. Boudreau, *Investing in People: Financial Impact of Human Resource Initiatives.* (Upper Saddle River, NJ: FT Press, 2008).

PG. 14 **... global business consultant KPMG found that its clients earned a return on investment (ROI) of 125 percent.** Riane Eisler *The Real Wealth of Nations: Creating a Caring Economics.* (Oakland, CA: Berrett-Koehler Publishers 2008).

PG. 14 **Studies show a healthy gender mix at the leadership level makes business smarter and more creative and improves its performance.** Katherine W Phillips, "How Diversity Makes Us Smarter: Being Around People Who Are Different From Us Makes Us More Creative, More Diligent and Harder-Working," *Scientific American* (October 1, 2014): accessed April 15, 2016. http://www.scientificamerican.com/article/how-diversity-makes-us-smarter/.

PG. 15 **A master in the art of living draws no sharp distinction between his work and his play ...** Lawrence Pearsall Jacks, *Education through Recreation (*New York: Harper & Brothers, 932), 1.

THREE PERSPECTIVES: THE HISTORY OF PATAGONIA'S ON-SITE CHILD-CARE PROGRAM

PG. 38 **Education is a natural process carried out by the child and is not acquired by listening to words, but by experiences in the environment.** Maria Montessori, *The Absorbent Mind* (Lanham, MD: Start Publishing, 2012), 7.

PART TWO

CHAPTER ONE: 33 YEARS OF LESSONS LEARNED

PG. 48 **A 1995 report revealed that most child-care programs in the United States were mediocre.** Suzanne W. Helburn and Carollee Howes, "Child Care Cost and Quality," Princeton University: accessed May 4, 2016. https://www.princeton.edu/futureofchildren/publications/docs/06_02_03.pdf.

PG. 48 **In 1996, a study provided insights into very young infants' learning capabilities connecting brain development and children's learning.** Julee J. Newberger, "New Brain Development Research—A Wonderful Window of Opportunity to Build Public Support for Early Childhood Education!" *Young Children* 52, no. 4 (May 1997): 4-9.

CHAPTER TWO: OUR PHILOSOPHY

PG. 53 **Childhood is not a race to see how quickly a child can read, write, and count. It's a small window of time to learn and develop at the pace that is right for each individual child. Earlier is not better.** Magda Gerber, "The Natural Child Project:" accessed on May 11, 2016, http://www.naturalchild.org/quotes/2013.html.

PG. 54 **As research mounted showing that mothers and infants benefit physically and emotionally from nursing, we developed systems that let families prolong nursing past the crucial first six months.** Jeannette Crenshaw, "Care Practice #6: No Separation of Mother and Baby, With Unlimited Opportunities for Breastfeeding." *Journal of Perinatal Education* 16, no. 3 (January 22, 2007): 39-43. doi:10.1624/105812407X217147.

PG. 55 **Businesses that provide paternity leave and encourage men to take advantage of it earn employee loyalty, boost retention rates, and have balanced, focused employees.** Eileen Appelbaum and Ruth Milkman, "Leaves That Pay: Worker Experience with Paid Family Leave in California." Center for Economic and Policy Research (2011): accessed April 13, 2016, http://cepr.net/documents/publications/paid-family-leave-1-2011.pdf.

PG. 55 **Dads report feeling engaged and happy when they care for their children from the start.** United States Department of Labor. "Paternity Leave: Why Parental Leave for Fathers Is So Important for Working Families," (June 17, 2015): accessed April 13, 2016, http://www.dol.gov/asp/policy-development/PaternityBrief.pdf.

PG. 55 **When parents both care for a newborn, their bonds deepen, and children benefit emotionally, socially, and cognitively.** Kate Fogarty and Garret D. Evans, "The Hidden Benefits of Being an Involved Father." The University of Florida (November 2009): accessed April 13, 2016, http://www.cfuf.org/Filestream.aspx?FileID=14.

PG. 55 **A recent study by Sarah Thébaud at the University of California, Santa Barbara, found that men and women ages 18 to 32, across all education and income levels, felt that men and women should share child raising. But when faced with a lack of family-friendly policies at work, most of them fell back on traditional roles.** Sarah Thébaud and David S. Pedulla. "Can We Finish the Revolution? Gender, Work-Family Ideals, and Institutional Constraint," *American Sociological Review* (February 2015): 116–39.

PG. 57 **Yvon Chouinard wrote in *The Responsible Company: What We've Learned from Patagonia's First 40 Years*, "The presence of kids and the introduction of child care taught us that if there is some quality about the workplace you love and don't want to lose, don't. It costs Patagonia $50,000, on average, to recruit, train, and get up to speed a new employee; if we want to make any money, it's a good idea to keep the ones we have happy and fully engaged."** Yvon Chouinard and Vincent Stanley, *The Responsible Company.* 1st ed. (Ventura, CA: Patagonia Books, 2012), 45.

PG. 59 **If adults consistently rescue children from safe but uncomfortable situations, children will rely on adult intervention and eventually learn to lack confidence in their abilities.** Anne Michaud, "The Terrible Downside of Helicopter Parenting." *Pittsburgh Post-Gazette* (February 5, 2015): accessed April 13, 2016, http://www.questia.com/read/1P2-38180919/the-terrible-downside-of-helicopter-parenting.

PG. 59 **Every test successfully met is rewarded by some growth in intuitive knowledge, strengthening of character, or initiation into a higher consciousness.** Paul Brunton, *Perspectives, Vol. 1: The Notebooks of Paul Brunton—A Survey of Categories 1–28* (New York: Larson Publications, 1984).

PG. 60 **When children make relatively small decisions, "Should I jump from this rock?" they practice assessing risk before they get older and must make higher-stakes choices.** Tim Gill, *No Fear: Growing Up in a Risk Averse Society.* (London: Calouste Gulbenkian Foundation: Distributed by Central Books, 2007).

PG. 61 **Unstructured play gives children the time they need to develop strong friendships and explore and master their interests, which leads to better problem-solving and social skills.** Kenneth R. Ginsburg, "The Importance of Play in Promoting Healthy Child Development and Maintaining Strong Parent-Child Bonds." The American Academy of Pediatrics (2007): accessed April 13, 2016, http://www2.aap.org/pressroom/playFINAL.pdf.

PG. 61 **Dr. Stuart Brown, a psychologist, and founder of the National Institute for Play, agrees that children need an environment with "the opportunity to engage in open, free play where they're allowed to self-organize. It's really a central part of being human and developing into competent adulthood. ... Wild play helps shape who we become. It should be embraced, not feared."** Eric Westervelt, "Play Hard, Live Free: Where Wild Play Still Rules." NPR Ed. National Public Radio (August 4, 2015): accessed April 13, 2016, http://www.npr.org/sections/ed/2015/08/04/425912755/play-hard-live-free-where-wild-play-still-rules.

Fall Catalog 2008 — Woods Wheatcroft

Fall Catalog 1986 — *Al Read*

PG. 62 **Karen Stephens, educator and champion of positive discipline, believes that "Valuable social skills are developed as children learn to problem solve and defuse confrontations. Logical thinking is nurtured as children comprehend rules and reasons for them. When experiencing consequences, children learn about cause and effect. They learn to anticipate and predict events within their control."** Karen Stephens, "What's so Positive about Positive Discipline?" Exchange Press (2003): 33.

PG. 63 **To punish children harshly dampens initiative and creativity, the qualities they need to flourish.** Wendy S. Grolnick, *The Psychology of Parental Control: How Well-Meant Parenting Backfires* (Mahwah, NJ: Lawrence Erlbaum Associates, 2003): accessed April 13, 2016, http://www.questia.com/read/110022497/the-psychology-of-parental-control-how-well-meant.

PG. 63 **Karen Stephens, expert on positive discipline, writes, "When positive discipline is used, caregivers introduce children to the world of relationships with compassion and patience. As a result, children develop social competence. Just as importantly, they learn to trust adults. By being treated with gentleness and high regard, they learn to respect and love themselves. All this is possible when teachers focus on positive practices."** Karen Stephens, "What's so Positive about Positive Discipline?" (Exchange Press, 2003), 33.

PG. 64 **Without the sound foundation of a healthy emotional life and the ability to connect with others, it's difficult for children to flourish in any educational environment.** Jennifer Kahn, "Can Emotional Intelligence Be Taught?" *New York Times*, September 11, 2013. Accessed April 13, 2016. http://www.nytimes.com/2013/09/15/magazine/can-emotional-intelligence-be-taught.html?pagewanted=all&_r=1.

PG. 64 **Research from the National Academy of Sciences and others indicates that "Young children who develop strong early relationships with parents, family, caregivers, and teachers learn how to pay attention, cooperate, and get along with others. They are confident in their ability to explore and learn from the world around them."** Lisa G Klein, "Set for Success: Building a Strong Foundation for School Readiness Based on the Social-Emotional Development of Young Children," *The Kauffman Early Education Exchange* 1, no. 1 (2002):6, accessed on May 4, 2016. http://sites.kauffman.org/pdf/eex_brochure.pdf.

PG. 64 **A friend is someone who gives you total freedom to be yourself.** Interview by Lizze James, "Jim Morrison: Ten Years Gone," *Creem* Magazine (1981): accessed May 9, 2016, http://archives.waiting-forthe-sun.net/Pages/Interviews/JimInterviews/TenYearsGone.html.

PG. 65 **Therefore, we've adapted and incorporated Louise Derman Sparks' goals for anti-bias curriculum.** Louise Derman-Sparks, *Anti-Bias Curriculum: Tools for Empowering Young Children.* NAEYC #242. (Washington, DC: National Association for the Education of Young Children, 1989).

PG. 65 **Diversity enhances creativity. It encourages the search for novel information and perspectives, leading to better decision making and problem solving.** Katherine W Phillips, "How Diversity Makes Us Smarter Being around People Who Are Different from Us Makes Us More Creative, More Diligent and Harder-Working." *Scientific American* (October 1, 2014): accessed April 18, 2016, http://www.scientificamerican.com/article/how-diversity-makes-us-smarter/.

PG. 66 **Young children are sensory creatures biologically wired to learn by taking action.** Alison Gopnik, "How Babies Think." *Scientific American* (July 2010): accessed April 13, 2016, http://www.alisongopnik.com/papers_alison/sciam-gopnik.pdf.

PG. 66 **Play that incorporates rich textural experiences allows children to express their emotions through manipulating the materials (clay, paint, sand) and refines their sense of touch. The richer the textural experiences, the richer their cognitive and language development will be ...** Liz Parnell, "The Importance of Messy Play." *Natural Child Magazine*: accessed May 9, 2016, http://www.naturalchildmagazine.com/0808/messy-play.htm.

PG. 67 **It is important to develop creativity at a young age. It may be that the attitude of being creative ...** M. Harrington, Jack Block, and Jeanne H. Block. "Predicting Creativity in Preadolescence from Divergent Thinking in Early Childhood." *Journal of Personality and Social Psychology* 45, no. 3 (1983): 609-23. doi:10.1037/0022-3514.45.3.609.

PG. 68 **When educators aren't treated with regard for their education, experience, and skill, teachers, children, and parents pay the cost.** Dave Eggers and Ninive Clements Calgari, "The High Cost of Low Teacher Salaries" *New York Times* (April 30, 2011): accessed April 13, 2016, http://www.nytimes.com/2011/05/01/opinion/01eggers.html?_r=0.

PG. 69 **We joyfully fight the trend observed by Professor Rhonda Clements that 70 percent of women who said they played outdoors every day as kids, reported that only 31 percent of their kids play outside daily.** Rhonda Clements, "An Investigation of the Status of Outdoor Play." *Contemporary Issues in Early Childhood* 5, no. 1 (2004): accessed April 22, 2016, http://www.imaginationplayground.com/images/content/2/9/2960/An-investigation-Of -The-Status-Of-Outdoor-Play.pdf.

PG. 70 **Joan Dye Gussow says, "Our uniquely American diets are rich in the wrong foods in bad proportions. Degenerative diseases take a long time to develop, but we know healthy eating equates to a healthy life."** Dan Barber quoting Joan Gussow in *The Third Plate: Field Notes on the Future of Food* (London: Penguin Books, 2014).

PG. 70 **To counter this, we follow the Mayo Clinic's advice by avoiding empty calories from added sugars, serving fruit-based desserts, and drinking water.** Jennifer K Nelson and Katherine Zeratsky, "Kids and Sugar—The Good, the Bad and the Ugly." Mayo Clinic (March 21, 2012): accessed April 13, 2016, http://www.mayoclinic.org/healthy-lifestyle/nutrition -and-healthy-eating/expert-blog/kids-and-sugar/bgp-20056149.

PG. 71 **Home is not a place. Home is security, predictability, reliability, dependability, safety, permanence, combined together.** Csaba Gabor-B, "Family and Values," *The Financialist* (August 8, 2013).

PG. 72 **The American Academy of Pediatrics recommends avoiding any screen time for children under two and advocates limiting the use of media technology for all children because hours of screen time lead to attention problems, school difficulties, sleep and eating disorders, and obesity.** American Academy of Pediatrics, "Media and Children:" (2016): accessed April 13, 2016, https://www.aap.org/en-us/advocacy-and-policy/aap-health -initiatives/pages/media-and-children.aspx.

PG. 73 **As Richard Louv writes in his book *Last Child in the Woods*, children who play in nature are an endangered species.** Richard Louv, *Last Child in the Woods: Saving Our Children from Nature-Deficit Disorder* (Chapel Hill, NC: Algonquin Books of Chapel Hill, 2008).

PG. 73 **Children should be taken to visit field, forest, hill, shore, the water, flowers, animals, the true homes of childhood. The very soul and body cry out for a more active, objective life and to know nature first hand.** Adapted from G. Stanley Hall quoted by Gary Ferguson. "Op-Ed: The Fear of the Great Outdoors," *Los Angeles Times*, (December 19, 2014): accessed April 13, 2016, http://www.latimes.com/opinion/op-ed/la-oe-1221-ferguson-humans-and -nature-20141221-story.html.

CHAPTER THREE: BUILDING RELATIONSHIPS

PG. 74 **An understanding heart is everything in a teacher ... One looks back with appreciation to the brilliant teachers, but with gratitude to those who touched our human feeling. The curriculum is so much necessary raw material, but warmth is the vital element for the growing plant and for the soul of the child.** C. G. Jung *The Development of Personality,* trans. R. F. C. Hull *(*London and New York: Routledge, Taylor & Francis, 1981), 144.

PG. 75 **The key to building children's strong relationships, with self and others, is positive connection—from birth—with trusted, caring adults.** S. Kontos and A. Wilcox-Herzog, "Research in Review: Teachers' Interactions with Children: Why Are They So Important?" *Young Children* 52, no. 2 (January 1997): 4–12.

PG. 77 **Students need to feel safe in order to take intellectual risks; they must be comfortable before they can venture into the realm of discomfort. Few things stifle creativity like the fear of being judged or humiliated.** Alfie Kohn, *Beyond Discipline: From Compliance to Community* (Alexandria, VA: Association for Supervision and Curriculum Development, 2006), 133.

Fall Catalog 1995 — *John Russell*

Spring Catalog 1990 — *Rick Ridgeway*

PG. 84 **Furthermore, research demonstrates that children do better academically and socially when their parents are involved in school, so child-care centers only win by welcoming parents.** A.T Henderson and K.L. Mapp. "A New Wave of Evidence: The Impact of School, Family, and Community Connections on Student Achievement." National Center for Family and Community Connections with Schools, Southwest Educational Development Laboratory (2002).

PG. 92 **The evidence increasingly points to an innate disposition [in children] to be responsive to the plight of other people ... Creating people who are socially responsive does not totally depend on parents and teachers. Such socializing agents have an ally within the child.** M. L. Hoffman, "Affect, Cognition, and Motivation: Empathy and Guilt," *Handbook of Motivation and Cognition: Foundations of Social Behavior*, ed. N. Eisenberg (New York: The Guilford Press, 1986), 244–80.

PG. 98 **Healthy relationships hinge on these emotional skills: Identifying and labeling one's feelings. Recognizing emotions in others. Responding appropriately to emotions.** Daniel Goleman, *Emotional Intelligence* (New York: Bantam Books, 2005).

PG. 99 **Research indicates that adults tend to talk about emotions more often with girls than with boys.** Daniel J. Kindlon, Michael Thompson, and Teresa Barker, *Raising Cain: Protecting the Emotional Life of Boys.* (New York: Ballantine Books, 2000).

PG. 100 **When teachers carefully observe children at play, they learn about children's feelings and can use that information to provide emotional support.** Ernie Dettore, "Children's Emotional Growth: Adult's Role as Emotional Archaeologists." *Childhood Education* 87, no. 5 (Summer 2002).

PG. 100 **As brain scientist Oliver Sacks wrote, "Very young children love and demand stories, and can understand complex matters presented as stories, when their powers of comprehending general concepts, paradigms, are almost non-existent."** Oliver Sacks, *The Man Who Mistook His Wife for a Hat and Other Clinical Tales.* (New York: Simon & Schuster, 1998), 184.

PG. 101 **Today, psychologists know that disingenuous praise makes children mistrust adults, shields kids from disappointment, and breeds low resilience.** Po Bronson, "How Not to Talk to Your Kids." *New York Magazine*, (August 3, 2007): accessed April 13, 2016, http://nymag .com/news/features/27840/index2.html.

PG. 102 **Insecurity can provide a moment for self-reflection.** Matthew Whoolery, "How to Lose Your Self-Esteem." TEDxRexburg (2015): accessed April 15, 2016, http://tedxtalks.ted .com/video/How-to-Lose-Your-Self-Esteem-Ma.

PG. 103 **If success means they are smart, then failure means they are dumb, that's the fixed mind-set.** Carol S Dweck, *Mindset: The New Psychology of Success* (New York: Ballantine Books, 2008), 175.

PG. 105 **In school, children learn to be citizens.** John Dewey, *Democracy and Education: An Introduction to the Philosophy of Education* (New York: Free Press, 1997).

PG. 105 **On the International Day of Peace ... join us in our celebrations and in making resolutions for each of us to do our part in working toward environmental sustainability. We cannot achieve the United Nations' Sustainable Development Goals unless we work together to make this a better world for people, other animals, and the environment.** Jane Goodall, "Dr. Goodall's Message for the 2015 United Nations International Day of Peace," Jane Goodall's Roots & Shoots, Jane Goodall Institute: accessed May 11, 2016, https://www. rootsandshoots.org/peaceday.

CHAPTER FOUR: INTENTIONAL ROUTINES

PG. 107 **Clear expectations and predictable sequences reduce power struggles and transform the mundane elements of life into meaningful rituals.** Zero to Three, "Love, Learning and Routines," Zero to Three: National Center for Infants Toddlers and Families: accessed April 14, 2016, http://www.zerotothree.org/child-development/social-emotional-development/love-learning-and-routines.html.

PG. 107 **"We not only respect [children] … we demonstrate our respect every time we interact with them. Respecting a child means treating even the youngest infant as a unique human being, not as an object."** Magda Gerber and Joan Weaver. *Dear Parent: Caring for Infants with Respect* (Los Angeles: Resources for Infant Educarers [RIE], 1998), 3.

PG. 116 **When diapering and dressing babies and toddlers, we use the RIE methodology, because we believe that these practices empower children.** Magda Gerber and Joan Weaver. *Dear Parent: Caring for Infants with Respect* (Los Angeles: Resources for Infant Educarers [RIE], 1998).

PG. 122 **According to pediatric specialist Dr. Kacie Flegal, if babies are barefoot, " … the little pads of babies' feet feel, move, and balance on the surface that they are exploring, the information sent to the brain from tactile, proprioceptive, and vestibular pathways quiet, or inhibit, other extraneous sensory input. This creates focus and awareness of walking and moving through space; babies get more tuned in to their surroundings."** Kacie Flegal, "Barefoot Babies," *Natural Child Magazine:* accessed April 14, 2016, http://www.naturalchildmagazine.com/1210/barefoot-babies.htm.

PG. 122 **Play gives children a chance to practice what they are learning.** Fred Rogers, Mister Rogers Talks With Parents. (Milwaukee, Wisconsin: Leonard Hal Pub Corp, 1993).

CHAPTER FIVE: CREATIVE PLAY

PG. 127 **Experts of all stripes have stated that play is an essential part of a healthy childhood.**

– Kenneth R. Ginsburg, "The Importance of Play in Promoting Healthy Child Development and Maintaining Strong Parent-Child Bonds." The American Academy of Pediatrics (2007).

– Office of the United Nations Commission on Human Rights, "Convention on the Rights of the Child," The United Nations Commission on Human Rights (September 2, 1990): accessed April 15, 2016, http://www.ohchr.org/en/professionalinterest/pages/crc.aspx.

– National Association for the Education of Young Children, "Developmentally Appropriate Practice in Early Childhood Programs Serving Children from Birth through Age 8: A Position Statement of the National Association for the Education of Young Children," National Association for the Education of Young Children (2009): accessed April 15, 2016, http://www.naeyc.org/files/naeyc/file/positions/PSDAP.pdf.

PG. 127 **According to pediatric occupational therapist Angela Hanscom, if children don't get enough unstructured playtime, "They are more likely to be clumsy, have difficulty paying attention, trouble controlling their emotions, utilize poor problem-solving methods, and demonstrate difficulties with social interactions."** Angela Hanscom, "The Decline of Play in Preschoolers and the Rise in Sensory Issues," *Washington Post* (September 1, 2015): accessed April 13, 2016, https://www.washingtonpost.com/blogs/answer-sheet/wp/2015/09/01/the-decline-of-play-in-preschoolers-and-the-rise-in-sensory-issues/.

PG. 127 **The very existence of youth is due in part to the necessity for play; the animal does not play because he is young, he has a period of youth because he must play.** Karl Groos, "Author Preface" in *The Play of Animals*, trans. Elizabeth L. Baldwin (New York: Appleton 1898), xvii–xviii.

PG. 129 **Children need to spend a large portion of their day outdoors to get the stimulation and natural learning experiences they are born to crave. We believe that hands-on experiential learning is the best educational approach for children. Being outdoors provides them with not only fresh air, it encourages imaginative play, creativity, hand-eye coordination, balance, physical strength and mental clarity.** Philosophy of the Field & Forest Outdoor Preschool: accessed May 22, 2016, http://www.atticoutdoorpreschool/Benefits.html.

PG. 130 **When adults support play in a skillful and subtle manner, play flourishes. If adults are too involved and directive, play deteriorates.** Rachel E. White, "The Power of Play: A Research Summary on Play and Learning," Minnesota Children's Museum (2012): accessed April 15, 2016, www.mcm.org/uploads/MCMResearchSummary.pdf.

Fall Catalog 1992 — Ace Kvale

PG. 134 **To combat this trend, we look to the adventure playground movement, founded 80 years ago by a Danish architect. Adventure playgrounds are stocked with wood, loose parts, and tools. Risk, ingenuity, and independence abound as kids built their own equipment.** Joe L Frost, *A History of Children's Play and Play Environments: Toward a Contemporary Child-Saving Movement* (New York: Routledge, 2010).

PG. 134 **Playing outside has a positive impact also on manual dexterity, physical coordination, tactile sensitivity and depth perception.** Valsquier, Elise, "Benefits of an Outdoor Preschool," Field & Forest Outdoor Preschool: accessed April 18, 2016, http://www.atticoutdoorpreschool.org/Benefits.html.

PG. 135 **Carl Jung astutely observed that "The creation of something new is not accomplished by the intellect but by the play."** Carl Gustav Jung *The Collected Works of C. G. Jung.* trans. , R. Hull, and H. G. Baynes (Princeton : Princeton University Press, 1971), 123.

PG. 135 **A child loves his play, not because it's easy, but because it's hard.** Benjamin Spock, *The Common Sense Book of Baby and Child Care.* (New York: Ishi Books, 2013), 247.

PG. 138 **"Kids now are the same as they ever were, and have been throughout time. They climb things, they hide in things, they create dens and places to hide in, create hierarchies and worlds of their own. They're drawn to fire, they're super-imaginative. What's different [today] is the degree to which they have an opportunity to express and pursue these interests. So it's surprising to us—but really it shouldn't be—that kids thrive in these environments when they can do really whatever they want. They have the play drive. It's up to us to kind of provide the kinds of opportunities for them to really follow through on it."** Erin Davis, writer, director, producer of *The Land.* Documentary, New Day Films (2015).

PG. 139 **Only the outdoors can provide the variety and stimulation of all the developing senses. Children initiating their own curiosity to explore and discover provides a personal relationship with their own feelings of competence in the natural world. Outdoors fosters resilient, independent, creative learners. The young explorer is stimulated with the "... ever-changing moods and marvels, potential and challenges of the natural world through the seasons."** "Ethos," Forest School Training The Principles of Forest Schools: accessed April 15, 2016, http://www.forestschooltraining.co.uk/ethos/.

PG. 140 **We also respect the stages of play: solitary, parallel, associative, and cooperative.** Rachel E White, "The Power of Play: A Research Summary on Play and Learning," Minnesota Children's Museum (2012): accessed April 15, 2016, www.mcm .org/uploads/MCMResearchSummary.pdf.

PG. 144 **According to a research summary by the Minnesota Children's Museum, "Despite the potential physical and cognitive benefits bestowed by physical activity, physical play is one of the least researched forms of play. It is also one of the most endangered forms of play in our schools and society: recess in schools is disappearing at an alarming rate and active play among youngsters has plummeted by 50 percent over the last 40 years."** Rachel E. White, "The Power of Play: A Research Summary on Play and Learning," Minnesota Children's Museum (2012): accessed April 15, 2016, www.mcm.org/uploads/MCMResearchSummary.pdf.

PG. 146 **Movement play lights up the brain and fosters learning, innovation, flexibility, adaptability, and resilience. These central aspects of human nature require movement to be fully realized.** Stuart L. Brown and Christopher C. Vaughan, *Play: How It Shapes the Brain, Opens the Imagination, and Invigorates the Soul.* (New York: Avery, 2009).

PG. 149 **The child amidst his baubles is learning the action of light, motion, gravity, [and] muscular force ...** Ralph Waldo Emerson, *The Essential Writings of Ralph Waldo Emerson,* ed. Brooks Atkinson (New York: Random House Publishing Group, 2000), 64.

PG. 151 **Play, while it cannot change the external realities of children's lives, can be a vehicle for children to explore and enjoy their differences and similarities and to create, even for a brief time, a more just world where everyone is an equal and valued participant.** Patricia G. Ramsey, Leslie R. Williams, and Edwina Battle Vold, *Multicultural Education: A Source Book* (New York: RoutledgeFalmer, 2003).

Summer Catalog 2012 — *Don King*

PG. 153 **'Pretend' often confuses the adult, but it is the child's real and serious world, the stage upon which any identity is possible and secret thoughts can be safely revealed.** Paley, Vivian Gussin, *The Boy Who Would Be a Helicopter* (Cambridge, MA: Harvard University Press, 1990), 7.

PG. 153 **Imagination is more important than knowledge. For knowledge is limited to all we know and understand while imagination embraces the entire world and all there ever will be to know and understand.** Albert Einstein and George Sylvester Viereck. "What Life Means to Einstein: An Interview by George Sylvester Viereck." Saturday Evening Post Society (October 26, 1929), *The Saturday Evening Post* edition, sec. Column 1: accessed May 22, 2016, www.saturdayeveningpost.com/wp-content/uploads/satevepost/what_life _means_to_einstein.pdf.

PG. 155 **Children use play as a form of imitation.** Jean Piaget, *Play, Dreams and Imitation in Childhood*. (New York: Norton, 1962), 102.

PG. 157 **Play energizes us and enlivens us. It eases our burdens. It renews our natural sense of optimism and opens us up to new possibilities.** Stuart L Brown and Christopher C. Vaughan. *Play: How It Shapes the Brain, Opens the Imagination, and Invigorates the Soul* (New York: Avery, 2009).

CHAPTER SIX: EXPLORING INDOORS AND OUTDOORS

PG. 159 **We may say that the adult works to perfect his environment, whereas the child works to perfect himself, using the environment as the means.** E. M. Standing, *Maria Montessori, Her Life and Work* (New York: Plume, 1998), 143.

PG. 161 **When [children] have enough space, safe space, they will do exactly the movements that they are ready for—because they have the opportunity.** Magda Gerber and Joan Weaver, *Dear Parent: Caring for Infants with Respect*. (Los Angeles: Resources for Infant Educators [RIE], 1998), 13.

PG. 162 **New research indicates that background noise can hinder how children learn. Experiments on speech perception done at University of North Carolina revealed that toddlers found noise more distracting than adults.** Neergaard, Lauran. "Noise Harder on Children than Adults, Hinders How They Learn," *Associated Press* (February 13, 2016): accessed April 14, 2016, https://www.yahoo.com/news/noise-harder-children-adults -hinders-191640113.html?ref=gs.

PG. 162 **Dr. Rochelle Newman of University of Maryland offers tips to "turn down the volume" and insure young children can focus and listen.** Neergaard, Lauran, "Noise Harder on Children than Adults, Hinder How They Learn," Associated Press (February 13, 2016): accessed April 14, 2016, https://www.yahoo.com/news/noise-harder-children-adults -hinders-191640113.html?ref=gs.

PG. 171 **A staple of the outdoor classroom, the messy kitchen is stocked with natural materials and household items.** Eric M Nelson, *Cultivating Outdoor Classrooms: Designing and Implementing Child-Centered Learning Environments* (St. Paul, MN: Redleaf Press, 2012).

PG. 173 **To evaluate our classrooms, we use the Infant Toddler Environment Rating Scale (ITERS), the Early Childhood Environment Rating Scale (ECERS) and School-Age Care Environment Rating Scale (SACERS).** Frank Porter Graham Child Development Institute, "Assessment Instruments for Early Childhood and Child Care Program Quality" (Chapel Hill: The University of North Carolina at Chapel Hill): accessed April 18, 2016, http://ers.fpg.unc.edu.

PG. 184 **Children need the freedom and time to play. Play is not a luxury. Play is a necessity.** Kay R. Jamison, *Exuberance: The Passion for Life* (New York: Vintage Books, 2005), 62.

Summer Catalog 2016 — *Spencer Suitt*

Chapter Notes

Fall Catalog 1987 — *John Russell*

CHAPTER SEVEN: LEARNING THROUGH OUR SENSES

PG. 187 **Everything [children] see, hear, feel, touch, or even smell impacts their brain and thus influences the way they view and interact with their world—including their family, neighbors, strangers, friends, classmates, and even themselves.** Daniel J. Siegel and Tina Payne Bryson, *No-Drama Discipline: The Whole-Brain Way to Calm the Chaos and Nurture Your Child's Developing Mind* (New York: Bantam, 2014).

PG. 189 **As Richard Louv writes, "Any natural place contains an infinite reservoir of information and, therefore, the potential for inexhaustible new discoveries."** Richard Louv, *Last Child in the Woods: Saving Our Children from Nature-Deficit Disorder* (Chapel Hill, NC: Algonquin Books of Chapel Hill, 2008), 68.

PG. 189 **Children live through their senses ... Since the natural environment is the principal source of sensory stimulation, freedom to explore or play with the outdoor environment through senses in their own space and time is essential for healthy development of an interior life.** Robin C Moore, "The Need for Nature: A Childhood Right," *Social Justice* 24, no. 3 (Fall 1997): 203.

PG. 190 **Psychologist Nancy Dess underscores the importance of human touch: "Without touch, infant primates die; adult primates with touch deficits become more aggressive."** Nancy Dess, quoted by Richard Louv, *Last Child in the Woods: Saving Our Children from Nature-Deficit Disorder* (Chapel Hill, NC: Algonquin Books of Chapel Hill, 2008), 67.

PG. 192 **Smell is the most primal human sense strongly connected to memory and emotion. The brain evolved from a pair of olfactory glands, so smell is an ancient sense connecting us to the rest of the animal kingdom. The nose is responsible for much of our sense of taste; it can pick up 10,000 more flavors than the tongue.** Ami Ronnberg and Kathleen Martin, *The Book of Symbols: Reflections on Archetypal Images* (Köln; London: Taschen, 2010), 362.

PG. 192 **Smell is a potent wizard that transports you across thousands of miles and all the years you have lived.** Helen Keller. *The Story of my Life* (Mineola: N.Y.: Dover Publications, 1996).

PG. 193 **The mouth is one of the first organs to appear in human embryos and continues to be primary in babies, who put items in their mouths to gather information.** Ami Ronnberg and Kathleen Martin, *The Book of Symbols: Reflections on Archetypal Images* (Köln; London: Taschen, 2010), 364.

PG. 194 **Humans are not born with a fully developed sense of sight. They can't control focus, eye movement, or use their two eyes in tandem.** American Optometric Association, "Infant Vision: Birth to 24 Months:" accessed April 14, 2016, http://www.aoa.org/patients -and-public/good-vision-throughout-life/childrens-vision/infant-vision-birth-to-24-months -of-age?sso=y.

PG. 199 **There is no inclement weather, only inappropriate clothing.** Alfred Wainwright and Derry Brabbs, *Coast to Coast Walk: A Pictorial Guide* (London: M. Joseph, 1987).

PG. 203 **All our knowledge begins with the senses.** Immanuel Kant, *Critique of Pure Reason*, 15. print. *The Cambridge Edition of the Works of Immanuel Kant*, trans. and eds. Paul Guyer and Allen W. Wood (Cambridge: Cambridge University Press, 2009), 1.

PG. 205 **The inexpressible depth of music, so easy to understand and yet so inexplicable, is due to the fact that it reproduces all the emotions of our innermost being.** Oliver Sacks, *Musicophilia: Tales of Music and the Brain* (New York: Vintage Books, 2008), xii.

PG. 206 **Research now shows that quality music programs teach children more than music. They improve reading, language, and math skills.** National Association for Music Education, "Research: Music Education and Brain Development:" accessed April 15, 2016, http://www.nafme.org/take-action/what-to-know/all-research/.

PG. 206 **Music is the universal language of mankind.** Henry Wadsworth Longfellow, *Outremer: A Pilgrimage Beyond the Sea* (Wildside Press, 2008), 4.

PG. 207 **A 2012 study of one-year-old infants found that interactive music classes lead to better communication.** David Gerry, Andrea Unrau, and Laurel J. Trainor, "Active Music Classes in Infancy Enhance Musical, Communicative and Social Development," *Developmental Science* 15, no. 3 (2012): 398.

CHAPTER EIGHT: INSPIRING CREATIVITY

PP. 208–237 This chapter is based on *Creative and Mental Growth* by Lowenfeld and Brittain. We are indebted to the work of both Viktor Lowenfeld and W. L. Brittain, and all quotes and concepts are from *Creative and Mental Growth*. Viktor Lowenfeld and W. Lambert Brittain, *Creative and Mental Growth*, 8th ed. (New York and London: Macmillan; Collier Macmillan, 1987).

CHAPTER NINE: STRENGTHENING BODIES

PG. 238 **Gross motor development happens naturally when an infant has plenty of space to move in a safe, age-appropriate, and challenging environment.** Stephanie Petrie and Sue Owen, eds., *Authentic Relationships in Group Care for Infants and Toddlers–Resources for Infant Educarers (RIE) Principles into Practice* (London and Philadelphia: J. Kingsley Publishers, 2005), 39.

PG. 239 **Each new skill–rolling over, sitting up, or crawling–lays the foundation in all areas of life: physically, mentally, and even socially.** Michael E. Lamb, Marc H. Bornstein, and Douglas M. Teti *Development in Infancy: An Introduction* (Mahwah, NJ: Lawrence Erlbaum, 2002): 130.

PG. 240 **Magda Gerber had the right idea. "Instead of trying to teach babies new skills, we appreciate and admire what babies are actually doing."** Magda Gerber and Joan Weaver *Dear Parent: Caring for Infants with Respect* (Los Angeles: Resources for Infant Educators (RIE), 1998), 3.

PG. 241 **Trust your baby's competence: she wants to do things for herself, and she can do things for herself.** Stephanie Petrie and Sue Owen, eds., *Authentic Relationships in Group Care for Infants and Toddlers–Resources for Infant Educarers (RIE) Principles into Practice* (London and Philadelphia: J. Kingsley Publishers, 2005), 41.

PG. 248 **Balance, the foundation of movement, is comprised of three elements: physical control, vision, and the awareness of the body in space–proprioception. The three systems develop slowly and in tandem.** Anne Shumway-Cook and Marjorie H. Woollacott, *Motor Control: Theory and Practical Applications.* (Philadelphia: Lippincott Williams & Wilkins, 2001).

PG. 254 **Swings are a gleeful way to try to touch the sky, and they play an important role in the growing child's body by stimulating the senses and the vestibular system.** Jill Mays, "The Vestibular System," *The Motor Story: An Inclusive Resource on Sensorimotor Development for Parents and Teachers*: accessed April 14, 2016, http://themotorstory.org/sensory-processing/the-vestibular-system/.

PG. 256 **Parents are four times as likely to tell girls than boys to be careful–according to a 2015 study in *The Journal of Pediatric Psychology*.** Elizabeth E. O'Neal, Jodie M. Plumert, and Carole Peterson, "Parent-Child Injury Prevention Conversations Following a Trip to the Emergency Department," *Journal of Pediatric Psychology* 41, no. 2 (March 2016): 256-64. doi:10.1093/jpepsy/jsv070.

CHAPTER TEN: WORKING WITH OUR HANDS

PG. 261 **During human evolution, increasingly complex use of tools evolved with thought and language–clearly conscious thought, language, and manual dexterity are interrelated.** Frank R Wilson, *The Hand: How Its Use Shapes the Brain, Language, and Human Culture* (New York: Vintage Books, 2013).

PG. 261 **The development of fine motor skills takes time and follows a predictable sequence.** Novella J Ruffin, "Understanding Growth and Development Patterns of Infants," Virginia Cooperative Extension: accessed April 14, 2016, http://pubs.ext.vt.edu/350/350-055/350-055.html.

Summer Catalog 2012 — *Kennan Harvey*

PG. 261 **The hand enjoys a privileged status in the learning process, being not only a catalyst but an experiential focal point for the organization of the young child's perceptual, motor, cognitive, and creative world.** Frank R Wilson, *All Work and No Play: How Educational Reforms Are Harming Our Preschoolers,* ed., Sharna Olfman, Childhood in America (Westport, CT: Praeger, 2003), 121.

PG. 262 **According to the National Center for Infants, Toddlers, and Families, "By mouthing and handling objects as a baby–safely, of course–she becomes "fluent" in ideas like side, edge, and corner. She doesn't have to "rediscover" blocks each time she plays. This enables your child to automatically apply this knowledge to solve more and more complex problems, like how to build a block tower."** Zero to Three, "Why Is My Child So Interested in Touching and Mouthing Toys?" "From Baby to Big Kid: Month 9," National Center for Infants Toddlers and Families: accessed April 14, 2016, http://www.zerotothree.org/child-development /play/qa/why-is-my-child-so.html.

PG. 263 **Before infants can use their hands, they must develop the hand-eye coordination needed to grasp things they want. Newborns can't control their gaze, but as their vision gets clearer, they see objects and people they want to reach for.** American Optometric Association, "Infant Vision: Birth to 24 Months:" accessed April 14, 2016, http://www.aoa.org /patients-and-public/good-vision-throughout-life/childrens-vision/infant-vision-birth-to-24 -months-of-age?sso=y.

PG. 273 **Puzzles tap into memory and problem-solving skills when children must remember that a piece that didn't fit in one place could now fit in another.** Pam Myers, "Why Puzzles Are Good for Your Child's Development." Child Development Institute, November 2, 2011. Accessed April 14, 2016. http://childdevelopmentinfo.com/child-activities/why-puzzles -are-good-for-your-childs-development/.

PG. 273 **Children astound me with their inquisitive minds. The world is wide and mysterious to them, and as they piece together the puzzle of life, they ask 'Why?' ceaselessly.** John C. Maxwell, *The Choice is Yours* (Nashville, Tennessee: Countryman* division of the Thomas Nelson Book Group, 2005).

CHAPTER ELEVEN: CONSTRUCTING MEANING

PG. 278 **Were all instructors to realize that the quality of mental process, not the production of correct answers, is the measure of educative growth, something hardly less than a revolution in teaching would be worked.** John Dewey, *Democracy and Education: An Introduction to the Philosophy of Education* (New York: Free Press, 1997, 207).

PG. 279 **Our thoughts are limited or expanded by the concepts and words we know, and research indicates that without language, we can't think even simple ideas like: *The object is located left of the blue wall*.** Jad Abumrad, and Robert Krulwich, "Words," Radiolab: accessed April 14, 2016, http://www.radiolab.org/story/91725-words/.

PG. 280 **Babies comprehend words before they produce them.** Paul C. Holinger, "Before Children Talk They Understand a Lot," *Psychology Today* (January 13, 2012): accessed April 14, 2016, https://www.psychologytoday.com/blog/great-kids-great-parents/201201 /children-talk-they-understand-lot.

PG. 281 **We speak not only to tell other people what we think, but to tell ourselves what we think.** Oliver Sacks, *Seeing Voices: A Journey into the World of the Deaf* (Berkeley: University of California Press, 1989), 19.

PG. 282 **Being able to communicate needs and desires reduces frustration and strengthens the bond between caregiver and infant.** Rachel H Thompson, Nicole M. Cotnoir-Bichelman, Paige M. McKerchar, Trista L. Tate, and Kelly A. Dancho, "Enhancing Early Communication through Infant Sign Training," ed., Louis Hagopian, *Journal of Applied Behavior Analysis* 40, no. 1 (2007): 15–23.

PG. 288 **John Dewey once said, "We only think when we are confronted by problems."** John Dewey, *How We Think* (Lexington, KY: Renaissance Classics, 2013).

Spring Catalog 1991 — *Pete Swart*

PG. 289 **One of the first ways that children use language to solve problems is by talking them-selves through the steps of a task.** L. S. Vygotskij, Eugenia Hanfmann, Gertruda Vakar, and Alex Kozulin, *Thought and Language.* Rev. and expanded ed. (Cambridge: MIT Press, 2012).

PG. 290 **Theorist Lev Vygotsky called this the "zone of proximal development." It refers to the range of activities and skills that children are ready to learn.** Lev Semenovich Vygotskij and Michael Cole, *Mind in Society: The Development of Higher Psychological Processes* (Cambridge, MA: Harvard University Press, 1981).

PG. 291 **Divergent problem solving is linked to creativity.**

-Robert R McCrae, "Creativity, Divergent Thinking, and Openness to Experience," *Journal of Personality and Social Psychology* 52, no. 6 (June 1987): 1258–65.

-Dennis. Hocevar "Intelligence, Divergent Thinking, and Creativity," *Intelligence* 4, no. 1 (1980): 25–40.

-Nina J Lieberman, "Playfulness and Divergent Thinking: An Investigation of Their Relationship at the Kindergarten Level," *The Journal of Genetic Psychology* 107 (1965): 219–24.

PG. 291 **Young children are naturally divergent thinkers, but tend to score lower on divergent problem-solving tests as they age.** Adrianus Hendrikus Wilhelmus van der Zanden, "The Facilitating University: Positioning next Generation Educational Technology" = De Faciliterende Universiteit: Positionering van Toekomstige Onderwijstechnologie, 2009, 252. http://site.ebrary.com/id/10852831.

PG. 292 **In the 1960s, psychologist Walter Mischel placed marshmallows in front of four-year-olds.** Walter Mischel, *The Marshmallow Test: Mastering Self-Control,* First edition (New York: Little, Brown and Company, 2014).

PG. 293 **The self is not something ready-made, but something in continuous formation through choice of action.** John Dewey, *Democracy and Education: An Introduction to the Philosophy of Education* (New York: Free Press, 1997), 408.

PG. 294 **Educator Vivian Paley once said that if you don't know your students' stories, then you don't really know your students.** Vivian Paley, "Who Will Save the Kindergarten? It Is Time to Reinvent the Garden of Children, and Only Their Teachers Can Come to the Rescue," presented at the NAEYCE Annual Conference, Orlando, FL, November 2, 2011.

PG. 294 **More recently, researchers also found that people who read fiction are more empa-thetic because reading about the internal lives of others teaches us to consider people's thoughts and motivations.** Juliet Chiaet, "Novel Finding: Reading Literary Fiction Improves Empathy: The Types of Books We Read May Affect How We Relate to Others," *Scientific American* (October 4, 2013): accessed April 14, 2016, http://www.scientificamerican.com /article/novel-finding-reading-literary-fiction-improves-empathy/.

PG. 296 **During the last few decades, the first-grade literacy curriculum has moved into kindergarten, and "educational" companies have marketed products that teach children to read at earlier ages.** Valerie Strauss, "Report: Requiring Kindergartners to Read—as Common Core Does—May Harm Some," *Washington Post* (January 13, 2015): accessed April 14, 2016, https://www.washingtonpost.com/news/answer-sheet/wp/2015/01/13/report-requiring -kindergartners-to-read-as-common-core-does-may-harm-some/.

PG. 296 **Despite years of research demonstrating no lasting benefit for early reading, the pressure on young children grows.** Sebastian P. Suggate, Elizabeth A. Schaughency, and Elaine Reese, "Children Learning to Read Later Catch up to Children Reading Earlier," *Early Childhood Research Quarterly* 28 (2013): 33–48.

PG. 296 **Children must be taught how to think, not what to think.** Geoffrey M. Horn, *Trailblazers of the Modern World: Margaret Mead* (Milwaukee, WI: World Almanac Library, 2004), 28.

PG. 297 **There is evidence that when children practice rhyming, they learn to read more easily—** perhaps because rhyming requires attention to sounds and syllables and develops phonemic awareness. P. E. Bryant, M. MacLean, L. L. Bradley, and J. Crossland, "Rhyme and Alliteration, Phoneme Detection, and Learning to Read," *Developmental Psychology* 26, no. 3 (1990): 429–38.

PG. 298 **The benefits of being able to speak, read, and write a second language include academic success and also the immeasurable benefit of being able to communicate and connect with those from other cultures.** Cody Delistray, "For a Better Brain, Learn Another Language." *The Atlantic* (October 17, 2014): accessed April 15, 2016. http://www.theatlantic .com/health/archive/2014/10/more-languages-better-brain/381193/.

PG. 298 In addition, **young children might have an easier time acquiring the sounds of language, which could result in better pronunciation.** Susan Oyama, "A Sensitive Period for the Acquisition of a Nonnative Phonological System," *Journal of Psycholinguistic Research* 5 (1976): 261-283.

PG. 299 **One language sets you in a corridor for life. Two languages open every door along the way.** Frank Smith, *To Think: In Language, Learning and Education* (London: Routledge, 1992).

CHAPTER TWELVE: TESTING THEORIES

PG. 303 **Young children think differently than adults.** Jean Piaget, *The Language and Thought of the Child.* Routledge Classics. (London: Routledge, 2001).

PG. 303 **Maria Montessori noticed that children's minds are inherently mathematical and that they are driven to classify and order reality.** Maria Montessori, *The Absorbent Mind* (Lanham, Maryland: Start Publishing, 2012). http://public.eblib.com/choice/publicfullrecord. aspx?p=1160838.

PG. 303 **Children have real understanding only of that which they invent themselves, and each time that we try to teach them something too quickly, we keep them from reinventing it them-selves.** Seymour Papert, "The Century's Greatest Minds: Papert on Piaget," Time Magazine (1999).

PG. 305 **Children explore chemistry through transformation.** Christine Chaillé and Lory Britain, *The Young Child as Scientist: A Constructivist Approach to Early Childhood Science Education* (Boston: Allyn and Bacon, 2003).

PG. 306 **The following guidelines from Developing Constructivist Early Childhood Curriculum help guide our practices:** *Developing Constructivist Early Childhood Curriculum: Practical Principles and Activities,* ed. Rheta DeVries (New York: Teachers College Press, 2002).

PG. 307 **Playing with physics is all about movement.** Christine Chaillé and Lory Britain, *The Young Child as Scientist: A Constructivist Approach to Early Childhood Science Education (*Boston: Allyn and Bacon, 2003).

PG. 308 **By observing flora and fauna, young kids engage with biology.** Christine Chaillé and Lory Britain, *The Young Child as Scientist: A Constructivist Approach to Early Childhood Science Education* (Boston: Allyn and Bacon, 2003).

PG. 310 **However, when you consider that math is defined as "… the science of numbers, quanti-ties, and shapes and the relations between them …"** "Mathematics," *Merriam-Webster Dictionary.* n.d.: accessed April 15, 2016, http://www.merriam-webster.com/dictionary/mathematics.

PG. 312 **Kids develop math skills by playing with quantity.** Eugene Geist, "Children Are Born Mathematicians: Promoting the Construction of Early Mathematical Concepts in Children Under Five," *Young Children* 56, no. 4 (July 2001): 12–19.

PG. 315 **The process of drawing, painting, or constructing is a complex one which children …** Viktor Lowenfeld and W. Lambert Brittain, *Creative and Mental Growth.* 8th ed. (New York and London: Macmillan; Collier Macmillan, 1987).

PG. 316 **Interestingly, English-speaking children have a difficult task because English doesn't have consistent rules about numbers. Think of the teens: 10, 11, and 12 do not have the word teen, like the rest of the sequence. In Chinese, the spoken words for numbers reflect the mathematical system, so 21 translates into two 10s plus one. The Chinese language reflects the pattern of numbers—in English this isn't the case.** Malcolm Gladwell, *Outliers: The Story of Success (*New York: Back Bay Books, 2008).

CHAPTER THIRTEEN: RAISING THE NEXT GENERATION

PG. 320 **Passion is lifted from the earth itself by the muddy hands of the young; it travels along grass-stained sleeves to the heart. If we are going to save environmentalism and the environment, we must also save an endangered indicator species: the child in nature.** Richard Louv, *Last Child in the Woods: Saving Our Children from Nature-Deficit Disorder.* (Chapel Hill, NC: Algonquin Books of Chapel Hill, 2008), 159.

PG. 321 **In 2015, a Stanford University study determined that walking outdoors in a park for one hour made the test subjects happier than walking for an hour in a city.** Gregory N. Bratman, Gretchen C. Daily, Benjamin J. Levy, and James J. Gross, "The Benefits of Nature Experience: Improved Affect and Cognition," *Landscape and Urban Planning* 138 (June 2015): 41–50.

PG. 321 **A recent study done in Amsterdam found that even images of natural settings can help students relax and improve their abilities in school.** Magdalena Van den Berg, Jolanda Maas, Rianne Muller, Anoek Braun, Wendy Kaandorp, René van Lien, Mireille van Poppel, Willem van Mechelen, and Agnes van den Berg, "Autonomic Nervous System Responses to Viewing Green and Built Settings: Differentiating Between Sympathetic and Parasympathetic Activity," *International Journal of Environmental Research and Public Health* 12, no. 12 (December 14, 2015): 15860–74.

PG. 321 **I only went out for a walk and finally concluded to stay out till sundown, for going out, I found, was really going in.** Sally M. Miller and Daryl Morrison, eds., *John Muir: Family, Friends, and Adventures* (Albuquerque: University of New Mexico Press, 2005), 153.

PG. 324 **Our forefathers were in daily contact with their environment.** Viktor Lowenfeld and W. Lambert Brittain, *Creative and Mental Growth,* 8th ed. (New York and London: Macmillan; Collier Macmillan, 1987), 13.

PG. 325 **When children need to run, jump, and climb, the best challenge is a landscape of grasses, rocks, and fallen trees. For quiet moments, turning over a rock reveals a diverse, alive ecosystem.** Richard Louv, *Last Child in the Woods: Saving Our Children from Nature-Deficit Disorder* (Chapel Hill, NC: Algonquin Books of Chapel Hill, 2008), 55–70.

PG. 326 **In Scandinavian countries, researchers found that children who play in natural landscapes tested better in motor development compared to those who play on flat playgrounds.** I. Fjortoft, "The Natural Environment as Playground for Children." *Early Childhood Education Journal* 29, no. 3 (2001): 111–17.

PG. 326 **School-age children asked to focus for longer periods of time need outdoor play to support classroom learning.** N. M. Wells, "At Home with Nature: Effects of 'Greenness' on Children's Cognitive Functioning." *Environment and Behavior* 32, no. 6 (n.d.): 775–95.

PG. 326 **According to the American Institutes for Research, "Studies in California and across the United States showed that schools that used outdoor classrooms and other forms of nature-based experiential education saw significant student gains in social studies, science, language arts, and math."** American Institutes for Research, "Effects of Outdoor Education Programs for Children in California," American Institutes for Research (January 27, 2005).

PG. 327 **The Outdoor Classroom.** "The Outdoor Classroom," The Child Educational Center (2015): accessed April 16, 2016, http://outdoorclassroomproject.org/about/the-outdoor-classroom/.

PG. 329 **"Those who contemplate the beauty of the earth find reserves of strength that will endure as long as life lasts."** eds., Lisa H. Sideris and Kathleen Dean Moore, *Rachel Carson: Legacy and Challenge. SUNY Series in Environmental Philosophy and Ethics* (Albany: State University of New York Press, 2008), 273.

PG. 331 **Anything else you're interested in is not going to happen if you can't breathe the air and drink the water. Don't sit this one out. Do something. You are by accident of fate alive at an absolutely critical moment in the history of our planet.** Carl Sagan quoted in Guy Dauncey, *The Climate Challenge: 101 Solutions to Global Warming* (British Columbia: New Society Publishers, 2009), 278.

Winter Catalog 2012 — Steve Ogle

Chapter Notes

Fall Catalog 2012 — *Jay Beyer*

PG. 333 Some people talk to animals. Not very many listen, though. That's the problem. Benjamin Hoff, *The Tao of Pooh* (New York: E.P. Dutton, 1982), 29.

PG. 334 There is nothing in a caterpillar that tells you it's going to be a butterfly. Buckminster Fuller, *I Seem To Be a Verb* (Berkeley: Gingko Press Inc., 2015).

PG. 335 Our campus is a certified monarch butterfly habitat. Monarch Watch, "Monarch Waystation Program:" accessed April 15, 2016, http://www.monarchwatch.org/waystations/.

PG. 337 Education's proper use is to enable citizens to live lives that are economically, politically, socially, and culturally responsible. A proper education enables young people to put their lives in order, which means knowing what things are more important than other things; it means putting first things first. Wendell Berry, *In the Presence of Fear: Three Essays for a Changed World* (Great Barrington, MA: Orion Society, 2001), 9.

PG. 340 Children connect with nature by going on field trips. Gerald A. Lieberman, and Linda L. Hoody, "Closing the Achievement Gap: Using the Environment as an Integrating Context for Learning," State Education and Environment Roundtable (Poway, CA: Pew Charitable Trusts, 1998): accessed April 15, 2016, http://www.seer.org/extras/execsum.pdf.

PG. 340 "For more effective education reform, teachers should free kids from the classroom." Richard Louv, *Last Child in the Woods: Saving Our Children from Nature-Deficit Disorder* (Chapel Hill, NC: Algonquin Books of Chapel Hill, 2008), 206.

PG. 343 He who plants a tree, plants a hope. Lucy Larcom in *Great Poems by American Women: An Anthology,* ed. Susan L. Rattiner (Mineola, NY: Dover Publications, 1998), 73.

PG. 347 I arise in the morning torn between a desire to improve the world and a desire to enjoy the world. E. B. White quoted in interview by Israel Shenker, "E. B. White: Notes and Comment by Author," *New York Times* (July 11, 1969): accessed May 10, 2016, http://www.nytimes.com/books/97/08/03/lifetimes/white-notes.html.

CHAPTER FOURTEEN: THE FUTURE

PG. 352 Journalist Alison Flood reveals, "'There is a shocking, proven connection between the decline in natural play and the decline in children's wellbeing ... Research found that a generation ago, 40% of children regularly played in natural areas, compared to 10% today, with a further 40% never playing outdoors. Obesity, anti-social behavior, friendlessness, and fear are the known consequences." Alison Flood, "Oxford Junior Dictionary's Replacement of 'Natural' Words with 21st-Century Terms Sparks Outcry," *The Guardian:* accessed May 16, 2016, http://www.theguardian.com/books/2015/jan/13/oxford-junior-dictionary-replacement-natural-words.

PG. 352 Leslie Paul founded the Woodcraft Folk in 1925, inspired by the work of Susan Isaacs in 1900. "Whole days in woodlands learning personal, social and technical skills provides natural self-regulated opportunities to develop confidence through hands-on learning." Liz O'Brien, Great Britain, and Forestry Commission, *A Marvellous Opportunity for Children to Learn: A Participatory Evaluation of Forest School in England and Wales* (Farnham, Surrey: Forest Research, 2006).

PG. 355 What Every Kid Should Be Able to Do by Age 16. "Go Simple, Go Solo, Go Now— The Life of Audrey Sutherland," The Cleanest Line, Patagonia (March 4, 2015): accessed April 20, 2016, http://www.thecleanestline.com/2015/03/go-simple-go-solo-go-now-the-life-of-audrey-sutherland.html?utm_content=buffer8ea9b&utm_medium=social&utm_source=twitter.com&utm_campaign=buffer.

ABUMRAD, JAD, AND ROBERT KRULWICH. "Words." Radiolab. Accessed April 14, 2016. http://www.radiolab.org/story/91725-words/.

AMERICAN ACADEMY OF PEDIATRICS. "Media and Children." American Academy of Pediatrics, 2016. https://www.aap.org/en-us/advocacy-and-policy/aap-health-initiatives/pages/media-and-children.aspx.

AMERICAN INSTITUTES FOR RESEARCH. "Effects of Outdoor Education Programs for Children in California." American Institutes for Research, January 27, 2005.

AMERICAN OPTOMETRIC ASSOCIATION. "Infant Vision: Birth to 24 Months." American Optometric Association, http://www.aoa.org/patients-and-public/good-vision-throughout-life/childrens-vision/infant-vision-birth-to-24-months-of-age?sso=y.

APPELBAUM, EILEEN, AND RUTH MILKMAN. "Achieving Workable Balance: New Jersey Employers' Experiences Managing Employee Leaves and Turnover." New Brunswick: Rutgers, n.d.

APPELBAUM, EILEEN, AND RUTH MILKMAN. "Leaves That Pay: Worker Experience with Paid Family Leave in California." Center for Economic and Policy Research, 2011. http://cepr.net/documents/publications/paid-family-leave-1-2011.pdf.

BARBER, DAN. *The Third Plate: Field Notes on the Future of Food*, 2014.

BERRY, WENDELL. *In the Presence of Fear: Three Essays for a Changed World*. Great Barrington, MA: Orion Society, 2001.

BLOOM, HAROLD. *Ralph Waldo Emerson*. New York: Chelsea House, 2007. http://public.eblib.com/choice/publicfullrecord.aspx?p=477494.

BORYSENKO, KARLYN. "What Was Management Thinking? The High Cost Of Employee Turnover." *Talent Management*, April 22, 2015. http://www.eremedia.com/tlnt/what-was-leadership-thinking-the-shockingly-high-cost-of-employee-turnover/.

BOUDREAU, JOHN W. *Investing in People: Financial Impact of Human Resource Initiatives*. Upper Saddle River, NJ: FT Press, 2011.

BOUSHEY, HEATHER, AND SARAH JANE GLYNN. "There Are Significant Business Costs to Replacing Employees." Center for American Progress, November 16, 2012. https://www.americanprogress.org/wp-content/uploads/2012/11/CostofTurnover.pdf.

BRATMAN, GREGORY N., GRETCHEN C. DAILY, BENJAMIN J. LEVY, AND JAMES J. GROSS. "The Benefits of Nature Experience: Improved Affect and Cognition." *Landscape and Urban Planning* 138 (June 2015): 41–50. doi:10.1016/j.landurbplan.2015.02.005.

BRONSON, PO. "How Not to Talk to Your Kids." *New York Magazine*, August 3, 2007. http://nymag.com/news/features/27840/index2.html.

BROWN, STUART L., TED Talk "Play is more than just fun, it's vital." Filmed May 2008. http://www.ted.com/talks/stuart_brown_says_play_is_more_than_fun_it_s_vital.

BROWN, STUART L., AND CHRISTOPHER C. VAUGHAN. *Play: How It Shapes the Brain, Opens the Imagination, and Invigorates the Soul*. New York: Avery, 2009.

BRYANT, P. E., M. MACLEAN, L. L. BRADLEY, AND J. CROSSLAND. "Rhyme and Alliteration, Phoneme Detection, and Learning to Read." *Developmental Psychology* 26, no. 3 (1990): 429–38. doi:10.1037/0012-1649.26.3.429.

BRUNTON, PAUL. *Perspectives, Vol. 1: The Notebooks of Paul Brunton—A Survey of Categories 1-28*. New York: Larson Publications. 1984.

CARSON, RACHEL, AND NICK KELSH. The Sense of Wonder. New York: Open Road Integrated Media, 2011.

CASCIO, WAYNE F., AND JOHN W. BOUDREAU. *Investing in People: Financial Impact of Human Resource Initiatives*. Upper Saddle River, NJ: FT Press, 2008.

CATALYST. "Women Leaving And Re-Entering The Workforce." Catalyst, March 28, 2013. http://www.catalyst.org/knowledge/women-leaving-and-re-entering-workforce.

CHAILLÉ, CHRISTINE, AND LORY BRITAIN. *The Young Child as Scientist: A Constructivist Approach to Early Childhood Science Education*. Boston: Allyn and Bacon, 2003.

CHIAET, JULIET. "Novel Finding: Reading Literary Fiction Improves Empathy: The Types of Books We Read May Affect How We Relate to Others." *Scientific American*, October 4, 2013. http://www.scientificamerican.com/article/novel-finding-reading-literary-fiction-improves-empathy/.

CHOUINARD, YVON, AND VINCENT STANLEY. *The Responsible Company*. 1st ed. Ventura, CA: Patagonia Books, 2012.

CHRISWICK, BARRY R., AND PAUL W. MILLER. "The Critical Period Hypothesis for Language Learning: What the 2000 US Census Says." *IZA Discussion Paper Series*. Bonn: Institute for the Study of Labor, 2007.

THE CLEANEST LINE. "Go Simple, Go Solo, Go Now – The Life of Audrey Sutherland." The Cleanest Line, Patagonia, March 4, 2015. http://www.thecleanestline.com/2015/03/go-simple-go-solo-go-now-the-life-of-audrey-sutherland.html?utm_content=buffer8ea9b&utm_medium=social&utm_source=twitter.com&utm_campaign=buffer.

COUNCIL OF ECONOMIC ADVERTISERS. "The Economics of Paid and Unpaid Leave." Executive Office of the President of the United States, Council of Economic Advisers, June 2014. https://www.whitehouse.gov/sites/default/files/docs/leave_report_final.pdf.

CRENSHAW, JEANNETTE. "Care Practice #6: No Separation of Mother and Baby, With Unlimited Opportunities for Breastfeeding." *Journal of Perinatal Education* 16, no. 3 (January 22, 2007): 39–43. doi:10.1624/105812407X217147.

DAHLBERG, GUNILLA, PETER MOSS, AND ALAN R. PENCE. *Beyond Quality in Early Childhood Education and Care: Postmodern Perspectives*. London and Philadelphia: Falmer Press, 1999.

DAUNCEY, GUY. *The Climate Challenge: 101 Solutions to Global Warming*. British Columbia: New Society Publishers. 2009.

DAVIS, ERIN. *The Land*. Documentary, 2015.

DELISTRATY, CODY. "For a Better Brain, Learn Another Language." *The Atlantic*, October 17, 2014. http://www.theatlantic.com/health/archive/2014/10/more-languages-better-brain/381193/.

DERMAN-SPARKS, LOUISE. *Anti-Bias Curriculum: Tools for Empowering Young Children*. NAEYC #242. Washington, DC: National Association for the Education of Young Children, 1989.

DETTORE, ERNIE. "Children's Emotional Growth: Adults' Role as Emotional Archaeologists." *Childhood Education* 87, no. 5 (Summer 2002).

DEVRIES, RHETA, ED. *Developing Constructivist Early Childhood Curriculum: Practical Principles and Activities. Early Childhood Education Series*. New York: Teachers College Press, 2002.

DEWEY, JOHN. *Democracy and Education: An Introduction to the Philosophy of Education*. New York: Free Press, 1997.

DEWEY, JOHN. *How We Think*. Lexington, KY: Renaissance Classics, 2013.

GOODALL, JANE. "Dr. Goodall's Message for the 2015 United Nations International Day of Peace." Jane Goodall's Roots & Shoots. The Jane Goodall Institute. Accessed May 11, 2016. https://www.rootsandshoots.org/peaceday.

left: Spring Catalog 1991 — *John Russell*

Spring Catalog 1992 — *David Brownell*

DWECK, CAROL S.. *Mindset: The New Psychology of Success*. Ballantine Books trade paperback. ed. New York: Ballantine Books, 2008.

EGGERS, DAVE, AND NINIVE CLEMENTS CALGARI. "The High Cost of Low Teacher Salaries." *New York Times*, April 30, 2011. http://www.nytimes.com/2011/05/01/opinion/01eggers.html?_r=0.

EINSTEIN, ALBERT, AND GEORGE SYLVESTER VIERECK. "What Life Means to Einstein: An Interview by George Sylvester Viereck." Saturday Evening Post Society. October 26, 1929, *The Saturday Evening Post* edition, sec. Column 1.

EISLER, RIANE. *The Real Wealth of Nations: Creating A Caring Economics*. BK Currents. San Francisco: Berrett-Koehler Publishers, 2008.

EMERSON, RALPH WALDO, AND BROOKS ATKINSON. *The Essential Writings of Ralph Waldo Emerson*. New York: Random House Publishing Group, 2000.

ENGLISH, LUCY, AND JAIME LADGE. "Enhanced Employee Health, Well-Being, and Engagement through Dependent Care Supports." Bright Horizons, n.d.

FJORTOFT, I. "The Natural Environment as Playground for Children." *Early Childhood Education* Journal 29, no. 3 (2001): 111–17.

FLEGAL, KACIE. "Barefoot Babies." *Natural Child Magazine*. Accessed April 14, 2016. https://www.naturalchildmagazine.com/1210/barefoot-babies.htm.

FLOOD, ALISON. "Oxford Junior Dictionary's Replacement of 'Natural' Words with 21st-Century Terms Sparks Outcry." *The Guardian*. Accessed May 16, 2016. http://www.theguardian.com/books/2015/jan/13/oxford-junior-dictionary-replacement-natural-words.

FOGARTY, KATE, AND GARRET D. EVANS. "The Hidden Benefits of Being an Involved Father." The University of Florida, November 2009. http://www.cfuf.org/Filestream.aspx?FileID=14.

FOREST SCHOOL TRAINING (FSTC). "ETHOS." FOREST SCHOOLS. The Principles of Forest Schools. Accessed April 15, 2016. http://www.forestschooltraining.co.uk/ethos/.

FRANK PORTER GRAHAM CHILD DEVELOPMENT INSTITUTE. "Environment Rating Scales." The University of North Carolina at Chapel Hill. Accessed April 18, 2016. http://ers.fpg.unc.edu.

FROST, JOE L. *A History of Children's Play and Play Environments: Toward a Contemporary Child-Saving Movement*. New York: Routledge, 2010.

FULLER, BUCKMINSTER. *I Seem to Be a Verb*. Gingko Press Inc., 2015.

GABOR-B, CSABA. "Family and Values." *The Financialist*, August 8, 2013.

GEIST, EUGENE. "Children Are Born Mathematicians: Promoting the Construction of Early Mathematical Concepts in Children Under Five." *Young Children* 56, no. 4 (July 2001): 12–19.

GERBER, MAGDA, AND JOAN WEAVER. *Dear Parent: Caring for Infants with Respect*. Los Angeles: Resources for Infant Educarers (RIE), 1998.

GERRY, DAVID, ANDREA UNRAU, AND LAUREL J. TRAINOR. "Active Music Classes in Infancy Enhance Musical, Communicative and Social Development." *Developmental Science* 15, no. 3 (2012): 398.

GILL, TIM. *No Fear: Growing Up in a Risk Averse Society*. London: Calouste Gulbenkian Foundation. Distributed by Central Books, 2007.

GINSBURG, KENNETH R. "The Importance of Play in Promoting Healthy Child Development and Maintaining Strong Parent-Child Bonds." The American Academy of Pediatrics, 2007.

GLADWELL, MALCOLM. *Outliers: The Story of Success*. 1st ed. New York: Back Bay Books, 2008.

GOLEMAN, DANIEL. *Emotional Intelligence*. 10th anniversary trade paperback. ed. New York: Bantam Books, 2005.

GOPNIK, ALISON. "How Babies Think." *Scientific American*, July 2010. http://www.alisongopnik.com/papers_alison/sciam-gopnik.pdf.

GROLNICK, WENDY S. "The Psychology of Parental Control: How Well-Meant Parenting Backfires." Mahwah, NJ: Lawrence Erlbaum Associates, 2003. http://www.questia.com/read/110022497/the-psychology-of-parental-control-how-well-meant.

GROOS, KARL. *The Play of Animals*, n.d.

HALL, G. STANLEY, AND GARY FERGUSON. "Op-Ed: The Fear of the Great Outdoors." *Los Angeles Times*, December 19, 2014. http://www.latimes.com/opinion/op-ed/la-oe-1221-ferguson-humans-and-nature-20141221-story.html.

HANSCOM, ANGELA. "The Decline of Play in Preschoolers and the Rise in Sensory Issues." *Washington Post*, September 1, 2015. https://www.washingtonpost.com/blogs/answer-sheet/wp/2015/09/01/the-decline-of-play-in-preschoolers-and-the-rise-in-sensory-issues/.

HARRINGTON, DAVID M., JACK BLOCK, AND JEANNE H. BLOCK. "Predicting Creativity in Preadolescence from Divergent Thinking in Early Childhood." *Journal of Personality and Social Psychology* 45, no. 3 (1983): 609–23. doi:10.1037/0022-3514.45.3.609.

HENDERSON, A.T., AND K.L. MAPP. "A New Wave of Evidence: The Impact of School, Family, and Community Connections on Student Achievement." National Center for Family and Community Connections with Schools, Southwest Educational Development Laboratory, 2002.

HEWLETT, SYLVIA ANNE, AND CYNTHIA BUCK LUCE. "Off-Ramps and On-Ramps: Keeping Talented Women on the Road to Success." *Havard Business Review*, March 2005. https://hbr.org/2005/03/off-ramps-and-on-ramps-keeping-talented-women-on-the-road-to-success.

HOCEVAR, DENNIS. "Intelligence, Divergent Thinking, and Creativity." *Intelligence* 4, no. 1 (1980): 25–40.

HOFF, BENJAMIN. *The Tao of Pooh*. New York: E.P. Dutton, 1982.

HOFFMAN, M.L. "Affect, Cognition, and Motivation: Empathy and Guilt." In *Handbook of Motivation and Cognition: Foundations of Social Behavior*, edited by N. Eisenberg, 244–80. New York: The Guilford Press, 1986.

HOLINGER, PAUL C. "Before Children Talk, They Understand a Lot." *Psychology Today*, January 13, 2012. https://www.psychologytoday.com/blog/great-kids-great-parents/201201/children-talk-they-understand-lot.

HORN, GEOFFREY M. *Trailblazers of the Modern World: Margaret Mead*. Milwaukee, WI: World Almanac Library, 2004.

JAMISON, KAY R. *Exuberance: The Passion for Life*. 1st Vintage Books ed. New York: Vintage Books, 2005.

JUNG, C. G. *The Collected Works of C. G. Jung*, Translated by R.F.C. Hull and H.G. Baynes. Princeton: Princeton University Press, 1971.

JUNG, C. G. *The Development of Personality*, Translated by R.F.C. Hull, 1981. http://public.eblib.com/choice/publicfullrecord.aspx?p=1573485.

Fall Catalog 1997 — *Rollie Ostermick*

Spring Catalog 1986 — *Rick Ridgeway*

KAHN, JENNIFER. "Can Emotional Intelligence Be Taught?" *New York Times*, September 11, 2013. http://www.nytimes.com/2013/09/15/magazine/can-emotional -intelligence-be-taught.html?pagewanted=all&_r=1.

KANT, IMMANUEL. *Critique of Pure Reason*. 15. print. *The Cambridge Edition of the Works of Immanuel Kant*, general ed.: and translated by Paul Guyer and Allen W. Wood. Cambridge: Cambridge University Press, 2009.

KENNY, ERIN K. Cedarsong Forest Kindergarten. Accessed April 14, 2016. http://cedarsongnatureschool.org/forestkindergarten/forest-kindergarten/.

KINDLON, DANIEL J., MICHAEL THOMPSON, AND TERESA BARKER. *Raising Cain: Protecting the Emotional Life of Boys*. 1st trade paperback. ed. New York: Ballantine Books, 2000.

KLEIN, LISA G. "Set for Success: Building a Strong Foundation for School Readiness Based on the Social-Emotional Development of Young Children." *The Kauffman Early Education Exchange*. Volume 1, number 1. 2002.

KOHN, ALFIE. *Beyond Discipline: From Compliance to Community*. 10th anniversary ed., 2nd ed. Alexandria, VA: Association for Supervision and Curriculum Development, 2006.

KONTOS, S., AND A. WILCOX-HERZOG. "Research in Review: Teachers' Interactions with Children: Why Are They So Important?" *Young Children* 52, no. 2 (January 1997): 4–12.

LAMB, MICHAEL E., MARC H. BORNSTEIN, AND DOUGLAS M. TETI. *Development in Infancy: An Introduction*. 4th ed. Mahwah, NJ: Lawrence Erlbaum, 2002.

LARCOM, LUCY. *Great Poems by American Women: An Anthology*. Edited by Susan L. Rattiner. Dover Thrift Editions. Mineola, NY: Dover Publications, 1998.

LIEBERMAN, GERALD A., AND LINDA L. HOODY. "Closing the Achievement Gap: Using the Environment as an Integrating Context for Learning." State Education and Environment Roundtable. Poway, CA: Pew Charitable Trusts, 1998. http://www.seer.org/extras/execsum.pdf.

LIEBERMAN, NINA J. "Playfulness and Divergent Thinking: An Investigation of Their Relationship at the Kindergarten Level." *The Journal of Genetic Psychology* 107 (1965): 219–24.

LOUV, RICHARD. *Last Child in the Woods: Saving Our Children from Nature-Deficit Disorder*. Updated and expanded. Chapel Hill, NC: Algonquin Books of Chapel Hill, 2008.

LOWENFELD, VIKTOR, AND W. LAMBERT BRITTAIN. *Creative and Mental Growth*. 8th ed. New York: London: Macmillan; Collier Macmillan, 1987.

"MATHEMATICS," n.d. http://www.merriam-webster.com/dictionary/mathematics.

MAYS, JILL. "The Vestibular System." *The Motor Story: An Inclusive Resource on Sensorimotor Development for Parents and Teachers* (blog). Accessed April 14, 2016. http://themotorstory.org/sensory-processing/the-vestibular-system/.

MAXWELL, JOHN C. The Choice *Is* Yours. Nashville, Tennessee: Countryman® division of the Thomas Nelson Book Group. 2005.

MCCRAE, ROBERT R. "Creativity, Divergent Thinking, and Openness to Experience." *Journal of Personality and Social Psychology* 52, no. 6 (June 1987): 1258–65.

MCKINSEY & COMPANY. "Women Matter: Female Leadership, a Competative Edge for the Future." McKinsey & Company, 2008. http://www.mckinsey.com/~/media/McKinsey /dotcom/client_service/Organization/PDFs/Women_matter_oct2008_english.ashx.

MICHAUD, ANNE. "The Terrible Downside of Helicopter Parenting." *Pittsburgh Post-Gazette*. February 5, 2015. http://www.questia.com/read/1P2-38180919/the-terrible-downside -of-helicopter-parenting.

MILLER, SALLY M., AND DARYL MORRISON, EDS. *John Muir: Family, Friends, and Adventures*. Albuquerque: University of New Mexico Press, 2005.

MISCHEL, WALTER. *The Marshmallow Test: Mastering Self-Control*. First edition. New York: Little, Brown and Company, 2014.

MONTESSORI, MARIA. *The Absorbent Mind*. Lanham, MD: Start Publishing, 2012. http://public .eblib.com/choice/publicfullrecord.aspx?p=1160838.

MOORE, ROBIN C. "The Need for Nature: A Childhood Right." *Social Justice* 24, no. 3 (Fall 1997): 203.

MORRISON, JIM. "JimMorrison: Ten Years Gone." Interview by Lizzie James in *Creem* magazine, 1981. Accessed May 9, 2016. http://archives.waiting-forthe-sun.net/Pages/Interviews /JimInterviews/TenYearsGone.html.

MYERS, PAM. "Why Puzzles Are Good for Your Child's Development." Child Development Institute, November 2, 2011. http://childdevelopmentinfo.com /child-activities/why-puzzles-are-good-for-your-childs-development/.

NATIONAL ASSOCIATION FOR MUSIC EDUCATION. "Research: Music Education and Brain Development." National Association for Music Education. Accessed April 15, 2016. http://www.nafme.org/take-action/what-to-know/all-research/.

NATIONAL ASSOCIATION FOR THE EDUCATION OF YOUNG CHILDREN. "Developmentally Appropriate Practice in Early Childhood Programs Serving Children from Birth through Age 8: A Position Statement of the National Association for the Education of Young Children." National Association for the Education of Young Children, 2009. http://www.naeyc.org /files/naeyc/file/positions/PSDAP.pdf.

NEERGAARD, LAURAN. "Noise Harder on Children than Adults, Hinders How They Learn." Associated Press. February 13, 2016. https://www.yahoo.com /news/noise-harder-children-adults-hinders-191640113.html?ref=gs.

NELSON, ERIC M. *Cultivating Outdoor Classrooms: Designing and Implementing Child-Centered Learning Environments*. 1st. ed. St. Paul, MN: Redleaf Press, 2012.

NELSON, JENNIFER K. AND KATHERINE ZERATSKY. "Kids and Sugar – The Good, the Bad and the Ugly." Mayo Clinic, March 21, 2012. http://www.mayoclinic.org/healthy-lifestyle /nutrition-and-healthy-eating/expert-blog/kids-and-sugar/bgp-20056149.

O'BRIEN, LIZ, GREAT BRITAIN, AND FORESTRY COMMISSION. *A Marvellous Opportunity for Children to Learn: A Participatory Evaluation of Forest School in England and Wales*. Farnham, Surrey: Forest Research, 2006.

O'BRIEN, SHARON. "My Willa Cather: How Writing Her Story Shaped My Own." *New York Times Book Review*, February 20, 1994.

OFFICE OF THE UNITED NATIONS HIGH COMMISSIONER FOR HUMAN RIGHTS. "Convention on the Rights of the Child." The United Nations Commission on Human Rights. September 2, 1990. http://www.ohchr.org/en/professionalinterest/pages/crc.aspx.

O'NEAL, ELIZABETH E., JODIE M. PLUMERT, AND CAROLE PETERSON. "Parent-Child Injury Prevention Conversations Following a Trip to the Emergency Department." *Journal of Pediatric Psychology* 41, no. 2 (March 2016): 256–64. doi:10.1093/jpepsy/jsv070.

Spring Catalog 1993 — *Yvon Chouinard*

THE OUTDOOR CLASSROOM PROJECT. "The Outdoor Classroom." The Child Educational Center, 2015. http://outdoorclassroomproject.org/about/the-outdoor-classroom/.

OWOCKI, GRETCHEN, AND LOIS BRIDGES BIRD. *Literacy Through Play*. Portsmouth, NH: Heinemann, 1999.

NATIONAL PARTNERSHIP FOR WOMEN AND FAMILIES. "Paid Leave." National Partnership for Women and Families, 2016. http://www.nationalpartnership.org/issues/work-family/paid-leave.html?

PALEY, VIVIAN GUSSIN. "Who Will Save the Kindergarten? It Is Time to Reinvent the Garden of Children, and Only Their Teachers Can Come to the Rescue." Presented at the NAEYC Annual Conference, Orlando, FL, November 2, 2011.

PALEY, VIVIAN GUSSIN. *Kindness of Children*. Cambridge: Harvard Univeristy Press, 2000. *The Boy Who Would Be a Helicopter*. Cambridge, MA: Harvard University Press, 1990.

PAPERT, SEYMOUR. "The Century's Greatest Minds: Papert on Piaget." *Time* magazine, 1999.

PARKER, KIM, AND WENDY WANG. "Modern Parenthood: Roles of Moms and Dads Converge as They Balance Work and Family." Pew Research Center, March 14, 2013. http://www.pewsocialtrends.org/2013/03/14/modern-parenthood-roles-of-moms-and-dads-converge-as-they-balance-work-and-family/.

PARNELL, LIZ. "The Importance of Messy Play." *Natural Child Magazine*. Accessed May 9, 2016. http://www.naturalchildmagazine.com/0808/messy-play.htm.

PETRIE, STEPHANIE, AND SUE OWEN, EDS. *Authentic Relationships in Group Care for Infants and Toddlers–Resources for Infant Educarers (RIE) Principles into Practice*. London and Philadelphia: J. Kingsley Publishers, 2005.

PHILLIPS, KATHERINE W. "How Diversity Makes Us Smarter: Being around People Who Are Different from Us Makes Us More Creative, More Diligent and Harder-Working." *Scientific American*, October 1, 2014. http://www.scientificamerican.com/article/how-diversity-makes-us-smarter/.

PIAGET, JEAN. *Play, Dreams and Imitation in Childhood*. New York: Norton, 1962.

PIAGET, JEAN. *The Language and Thought of the Child*. Routledge Classics. London: Routledge, 2001.

RAMSEY, PATRICIA G., LESLIE R. WILLIAMS, AND EDWINA BATTLE VOLD. *Multicultural Education: A Source Book*. 2nd ed. Source Books on Education Series. New York: Routledge Falmer, 2003.

ROGERS, FRED. *Mister Rogers Talks with Parents*. Hal Leonard Publishing Corp., 1993.

RONNBERG, AMI, AND KATHLEEN MARTIN. *The Book of Symbols: Reflections on Archetypal Images*. Köln; London: Taschen, 2010.

RUFFIN, NOVELLA J. "Understanding Growth and Development Patterns of Infants." Virginia Cooperative Extension. Accessed April 14, 2016. http://pubs.ext.vt.edu/350/350-055/350-055.html.

SACKS, OLIVER. *Musicophilia: Tales of Music and the Brain*. Rev. and expanded, 1st Vintage Books ed. New York: Vintage Books, 2008.

SACKS, OLIVER. *Seeing Voices: A Journey into the World of the Deaf*. Berkeley: University of California Press, 1989.

SACKS, OLIVER. *The Man Who Mistook His Wife for a Hat and Other Clinical Tales*. 1st Touchstone ed. New York: Simon & Schuster, 1998.

SEBASTIAN P. SUGGATE, ELIZABETH A. SCHAUGHENCY, AND ELAINE REESE. "Children Learning to Read Later Catch up to Children Reading Earlier." *Early Childhood Research Quarterly* 28 (2013): 33-48.

SHUMWAY-COOK, ANNE, AND MARJORIE H. WOOLLACOTT. *Motor Control: Theory and Practical Applications*. 2nd ed. Philadelphia: Lippincott Williams & Wilkins, 2001.

SIDERIS, LISA H., AND KATHLEEN DEAN MOORE, EDS. *Rachel Carson: Legacy and Challenge*. SUNY Series in Environmental Philosophy and Ethics. Albany: State University of New York Press, 2008.

SIEGEL, DANIEL J., AND TINA PAYNE BRYSON. *No-Drama Discipline: The Whole-Brain Way to Calm the Chaos and Nurture Your Child's Developing Mind*. First edition. New York: Bantam, 2014.

SMITH, FRANK. *To Think: In Language, Learning and Education*. London: Routledge, 1992.

SPOCK, BENJAMIN. *The Common Sense Book of Baby and Child Care*. New York: Ishi Books, 2013.

STANDING, E. M. *Maria Montessori: Her Life and Work*. New York: Plume, 1998.

STEPHEN, KAREN. "What's so Positive about Positive Discipline?" Exchange Press, 2003.

STRAUSS, VALERIE. "Report: Requiring Kindergartners to Read – as Common Core Does – May Harm Some." *Washington Post*, January 13, 2015. https://www.washingtonpost.com/news/answer-sheet/wp/2015/01/13/report-requiring-kindergartners-to-read-as-common-core-does-may-harm-some/.

THÉBAUD, SARAH, AND DAVID S. PEDULLA. "Can We Finish the Revolution? Gender, Work-Family Ideals and Institutional Constraint." *American Sociological Review*, February 2015, 116-39.

THOMPSON, RACHEL H., NICOLE M. COTNOIR-BICHELMAN, PAIGE M. MCKERCHAR, TRISTA L. TATE, AND KELLY A. DANCHO. "Enhancing Early Communication through Infant Sign Training." Edited by Louis Hagopian. *Journal of Applied Behavior Analysis* 40, no. 1 (2007): 15-23.

UNITED STATES DEPARTMENT OF LABOR. "Paternity Leave: Why Parental Leave for Fathers Is So Important for Working Families," June 17, 2015. http://www.dol.gov/asp/policy-development/PaternityBrief.pdf.

VALSQUIER, ELISE. "Benefits of an Outdoor Preschool." Field and Forest Outdoor Preschool. Accessed April 18, 2016. http://www.atticoutdoorpreschool.org/Benefits.html.

VAN DEN BERG, MAGDALENA, JOLANDA MAAS, RIANNE MULLER, ANOEK BRAUN, WENDY KAANDORP, RENÉ VAN LIEN, MIREILLE VAN POPPEL, WILLEM VAN MECHELEN, AND AGNES VAN DEN BERG. "Autonomic Nervous System Responses to Viewing Green and Built Settings: Differentiating Between Sympathetic and Parasympathetic Activity." *International Journal of Environmental Research and Public Health* 12, no. 12 (December 14, 2015): 15860-74. doi:10.3390/ijerph121215026.

VYGOTSKI, L. S., EUGENIA HANFMANN, GERTRUDA VAKAR, AND ALEX KOZULIN. *Thought and Language*. Rev. and expanded ed. Cambridge, MA: MIT Press, 2012.

VYGOTSKIJ, LEV SEMENOVICH, AND MICHAEL COLE. *Mind in Society: The Development of Higher Psychological Processes*. Nachdr. Cambridge, MA: Harvard University Press, 1981.

WAINWRIGHT, ALFRED, AND DERRY BRABBS. *A Coast to Coast Walk: A Pictorial Guide*. London: M. Joseph, 1987.

WELLS, N.M. "At Home with Nature: Effects of 'Greenness' on Children's Cognitive Functioning." *Environment and Behavior* 32, no. 6 (n.d.): 775-95.

WESTERVELT, ERIC. "Play Hard, Live Free: Where Wild Play Still Rules." NPR Ed. National Public Radio, August 4, 2015. http://www.npr.org/sections/ed/2015/08/04/425912755 /play-hard-live-free-where-wild-play-still-rules.

WHITE, E. B. "E. B. White: Notes and Comment by Author." Interview by Israel Shenker. *New York Times*, July 11, 1969. Accessed May 10th 2016, http://www.nytimes.com/ books/97/08/03/lifetimes/white-notes.html.

WHITE, RACHEL E. "The Power of Play a Research Summary on Play and Learning." Minnesota Children's Museum, 2012. www.mcm.org/uploads/MCMResearchSummary.pdf.

WHOOLERY, MATTHEW. "How to Lose Your Self-Esteem." TEDxRexburg, 2015.

WILSON, FRANK R. *All Work and No Play: How Educational Reforms Are Harming Our Preschoolers*. Edited by Sharna Olfman. *Childhood in America*. Westport, CT: Praeger, 2003.

WILSON, FRANK R. *The Hand: How Its Use Shapes the Brain, Language, and Human Culture*. New York: Vintage Books, 2013. http://search.ebscohost.com /login.aspx?direct=true&scope=site&db=nlebk&db=nlabk&AN=727661.

ZANDEN, ADRIANUS HENDRIKUS WILHELMUS VAN DER. "The Facilitating University: Positioning next Generation Educational Technology" = De Faciliterende Universiteit : Positionering van Toekomstige Onderwijstechnologie, 2009. http://site.ebrary.com/id/10852831.

ZERO TO THREE. "Love, Learning and Routines." Zero to Three: National Center for Infants Toddlers and Families. Accessed April 14, 2016. http://www.zerotothree.org /child-development/social-emotional-development/love-learning-and-routines.html.

ZERO TO THREE. "Why Is My Child so Interested in Touching and Mouthing Toys? *From* Baby to Big Kid: Month 9." National Center for Infants Toddlers and Families. Zero to Three. Accessed April 14, 2016. http://www.zerotothree.org/child-development/play/qa/why-is-my -child-so.html.

A child's world is fresh and new and beautiful, full of wonder and excitement. — *Rachel Carson*

Spring Catalog 1989 — *Rick Ridgeway*

Spring Catalog 1988 — *John Russell*

left: **Fall Catalog 1995** — *Debbie Blehert-Koehn*

Spring Catalog 2016 — *Steve Ogle*

Summer Catalog 2015 — *Bernd Zeugswetter*

Fall Catalog 1996 — Andy Anderson

I sincerely believe that for the child, and
for the parent seeking to guide him, it
is not half so important to know as to feel
when introducing a young child to the
natural world. If facts are the seeds that
later produce knowledge and wisdom,
then the emotions and the impressions
of the senses are the fertile soil in which
the seeds must grow. The years of early
childhood are the time to prepare the soil.

— *Rachel Carson*

Fall Catalog 1998 — *Uli Wiesmeier*

All Done!